# Never Give Up!

*How I Survived a Heart Transplant, Multiple Heart Surgeries, Colon Cancer, a Coma, and Acute Thrombosis:*

## The Six Secret Steps You Must Take To Protect Your Own Life

### By Richard and Joan Stevens with Michael Levin

iUniverse, Inc.
New York   Bloomington

Never Give Up!
How I Survived a Heart Transplant, Multiple Heart Surgeries,
Colon Cancer, a Coma, and Acute Thrombosis: The Six Secret
Steps You Must Take To Protect Your Own Life

iUniverse books may be ordered through booksellers or by contacting:

iUniverse
1663 Liberty Drive
Bloomington, IN 47403
www.iuniverse.com
1-800-Authors (1-800-288-4677)

Because of the dynamic nature of the Internet, any Web addresses or
links contained in this book may have changed since publication and
may no longer be valid. The views expressed in this work are solely those
of the author and do not necessarily reflect the views of the publisher,
and the publisher hereby disclaims any responsibility for them.

ISBN: 978-1-4401-1932-3 (pbk)
ISBN: 978-1-4401-1933-0 (ebk)

Printed in the United States of America

iUniverse rev. date: 2/11/2009

I dedicate this book with great love and affection to the two
most magnificent women in my life:

To my wife, Joan, I owe everything. Her love and unwavering
support over the years enabled me to survive my ordeal.

To our daughter, Sandy: There are no words to convey what her
steadfast love meant during some very difficult times. She was
always there to support Joan and to do whatever was needed.

God sent me two angels right from my own family, and I am
eternally grateful.

Richard S. Stevens
2008

# Acknowledgments

A special thank you and undying affection for those who, through their medical skills, have been able to sustain my life. The following individuals and their associates have been almost daily companions for seven or eight years now, and have never failed me in providing the best of medical counsel and expertise: Dr. Mark Barr and Felicia Barr, Dr. Fred Weaver, Dr. Uri Elkayam, Dr. Virginia Cooke, Dr. Vaughn Starnes, and Dr. John Storch.

I would be remiss if I were not to recognize the many friends and family members who have contributed much to my well-being. These include my son Christopher, son-in-law Pete Weston, stepdaughter Lisa Levine, stepson Brad Levine, and many of my business associates, such as Bob Liljenwall, who have been unfailingly there for me when I needed them. Of course, we relied heavily on my friends Con Schweitzer, Wally Gayner and Landon Exley to keep my spirits up, and Ben and Barbara Harris just to be there at the right time. I had my Special Angel, Kara Fox, who would drive for hours just to be there when I most needed it. Our neighbors, Mary Stanley, Pat Ting, and Elie Polk ably handled our home needs so that Joan could be with me. Throughout all of it, we were supported by my outstanding assistant, Diane Ruhlander.

And then there is Dr. Lanny Taub, who personifies my theme of "Never Give Up!" He and his brother, Dr. Ed, have been effectively active for decades in creating Wellness as a growing medical tool. The Taubs have given their time and talent in helping me with this book, and for that, we are extremely grateful.

# Contents

# Chapter One:
# A Second Chance

I didn't know that I had died. I wasn't planning on it. Just before it happened, I was standing in line at the San Diego airport waiting to catch a flight home to Arizona. I was at the tail end of a fishing trip with some of my buddies in Mexico, where I'd felt in top form and had a fantastic time. My friends dropped me off at the airport in San Diego for my flight and continued on to their homes in Newport Beach, clueless as to what was about to happen to me.

I was standing in line, and suddenly, I dropped like a fallen oak tree. Later, I learned that a security guard who happened to be nearby knew CPR very well and began administering it as soon as I went down. He kept working on me for several minutes while someone called the paramedics. I'm sure it ran through his mind many times that, since I'd been out for well over ten minutes, the likelihood of me coming back was slim. He also must have been well aware that the brain almost always sustains major injury if it goes without oxygen for more than two or three minutes. But he kept working on me faithfully, and I'm extremely grateful.

Luckily, the University of California San Diego Hospital is located just fifteen minutes from the airport, and within a half hour, I was on my way there—Code Blue, with all sirens blaring. They later told me that my upper body had turned blue and that I was flatlining—meaning there were no appreciable signs of life in my body. Of course, I knew nothing of this. I saw no light at the end of the tunnel, heard no voices from the "great beyond," nothing. Just darkness.

My wife Joan had been attending a seminar in Arizona with our daughter Lisa, and when she got home, there was an emergency call waiting for her from the hospital. The doctor told her that I was unconscious and that the problem that laid me out arose from having low electrolytes in my system. They didn't know whether I would come out of it at all, and they offered no hope to Joan; they simply urged her to get to San Diego as soon as possible. She and Lisa commandeered emergency seats on the next flight out of Phoenix, and a short time later, they were in San Diego. The doctors were very succinct and brutal. They told my wife not to count on my ever coming out of the coma, and that even if I did, there was a high probability that I would be a vegetable for the rest of my life.

But the gods were with me. After forty-eight hours, I came out of a sustained coma to find myself in the hospital with my wife and daughter Sandy beside me. Joan was reading to me, and Lisa, our other daughter, was massaging my feet. Miraculously, I didn't seem to be much the worse for wear, other than short-term memory loss. I was not only able to get better, but was released from the hospital within a matter of a few days with a new defibrillator in my gut.

Dramatic recovery, you say? Absolutely! Am I lucky to be alive? Several times over. When I got out of the San Diego Hospital reasonably intact, I began to reflect on the amazing convergence of factors that kept me alive. If I'd had my attack two hours earlier, I would have been in Mexico, and dead meat. An hour later and I would have been on the plane, in midflight, and far from help. So who was looking after me that I happened to collapse at the ticket counter, within reach of a CPR-certified Good Samaritan and just minutes away from a wonderful hospital team? Why was I allowed to live? Perhaps writing this book is the reason.

Thanks to excellent medical care and the love and support of my family, I'm here to share my story with you, in the hopes that it will help you keep going, no matter what. If you've picked up this book, you or someone you know is likely facing significant medical treatment and even an extended stay in a hospital. Perhaps, God forbid, my story strikes a familiar chord. I want to show you what this and other experiences with health emergencies have taught me: that nothing is impossible if you have tremendous faith, combined with great medical care, a positive attitude, and loved ones who simply don't give up, either.

My brush with death in the San Diego airport was neither my first, nor my last. But surprisingly enough, I've come to realize that experiences like mine are not altogether uncommon, especially as our country faces increasing rates of heart disease and other illnesses that can strike swiftly and without warning. One out of five Americans will die from a heart attack or heart disease. Even as these threats are on the rise, I discovered, over the course of my struggle with heart disease, that the information available to me was limited. There are certainly medical texts out there, but what about the layperson? There has been very little written about catastrophic illness, and heart transplantation in particular, from the patient's standpoint.

In this book, you'll find a survival manual, written from one patient to another. This is not the sterile, detached advice of a doctor—though there's certainly a time and place for that. This is the grit and grime true story of someone who's been in the trenches. What I'm sharing with you is in no way intended to replace or subvert the advice of trained and skilled medical professionals. Instead, I hope to offer you a different perspective, the perspective of a survivor, to empower you to join your medical team in taking charge of your own well-being. I call these concepts "Dick's Rules." They saved my life ... and they can save yours, too!

In addition, I want to share some ideas with you about *how to avoid needing hospitalization in the first place.* We're all familiar with the old bromide of "an ounce of prevention is worth a pound of cure." There are things you can do—beyond the usual prescriptions of proper diet and regular exercise—that will minimize or perhaps even eliminate the possibility that you will end up in the same position I did, literally at death's door, years before your time. We all have to go sometime, as the expression goes, but you don't have to go at 47 or 52 or 61, from a heart attack, a stroke, or in some other horrific, untimely manner. I will share with you in this book the steps you can take *right now* to ensure your health and to be prepared in the event that some untoward event does occur.

Three life-changing events played a vital role in the development of my guidelines for hospital patients—and those who wish to avoid needing the hospital in the first place. The first was my father's sudden death from a heart attack at age forty-eight. I was twelve at the time, and his passing meant I had to grow up very quickly. I learned to take responsibility for myself, and along the way, I gathered that my own life expectancy would no doubt be quite short, since heart disease ran in my family. It was 1942, and the first successful heart bypass surgery, by legendary surgeon Dr. Michael DeBakey, was still twenty-two years away.

Thirty-nine years passed before my next life-altering incident. By that time, I was a successful corporate turnaround executive. Convinced that I would suffer the same fate as my dad, I had adopted a day-to-day lifestyle that included working and playing equally hard. I became a millionaire who also happened to be a hard-drinking, hard-partying playboy. At age forty-nine, just a year older than my dad was when he died, I suffered my first heart attack after playing a set of tennis. Unlike my father, however, I survived, primarily because I'd been born in a different generation. In fact, over the next twenty-seven years, I would survive four more heart attacks, endure two major heart bypass operations, and undergo several other heart-related surgeries due to complications like infections and blood clots. Doctors and hospitals became a major part of my life. The third life-changing event was my heart transplant in 2000. I spent four months in the hospital on my back, hooked up to an I.V., waiting for my new heart, a period of time when I developed, out of necessity, the principles I'll share with you in this book. Every time I heard the whir of helicopter rotors, indicating that a heart was arriving for a transplant patient, my spirits would soar, only to be dashed again when I realized the heart was not meant for me. Eventually I learned that, by the time your heart is on its way, you're already under sedation for the transplant operation, so I stopped having those moments of hope followed by despair. I'll talk more about these experiences later in the book.

These episodes occurred over a span of fifty-eight years, and when you consider the advances in heart treatment technology in that relatively short time, it's mind-boggling. In my father's day, heart bypass surgery, defibrillators and heart transplants simply did not exist—but these are the advancements that have kept me alive.

After my first attack, I became a recipient of these state-of-the-art treatments, and the fortunate beneficiary of an extended life. Each time my body seemed to be on the brink of breaking down, there was another life-saving procedure to bail me out. But as I spent more time in hospitals, I learned that these institutions aren't the smooth-running operations I had built a career on creating in the business world—far from it! Resources are tight; doctors, nurses, and technicians are overworked; mistakes happen. My medical journey makes me think of a mouse trying to find its way through a maze, with a close call at every turn. For all the technology and skill used to keep patients alive, the medical profession is still deficient in guiding its patients through the process and educating them on the hazards that lie ahead. There is no cure for human error and carelessness, and therefore, no place for passiveness on the part of the patient and the people charged with overseeing his or her care, even in a country blessed with the finest doctors and medical technology in the world.

I'll use examples from my own experience throughout this book to illustrate the importance of each element of the plan

I created for navigating the health care system. This plan is deceptively simple, but don't underestimate the power of clear, simple ideas. These concepts may just save your life, just as they saved mine!

You'll come to know my story well, and it is my hope that my story will shed some light on your own. I'll start by telling you how, with my father's death, I was abruptly and harshly initiated into the uncertain world of living with a serious and unpredictable medical condition.

On Christmas Day, 1942, my dad suffered a heart attack. I remember walking into his bedroom as my mother was on the phone with our doctor. Dad was lying on his back, staring at the ceiling. He looked at me and waved me over to the side of his bed. His breathing was heavy, his face as ashen as an overcast midday sky. He raised his right hand and motioned with his fingers, urging me closer. I leaned over and gripped his hand in mine.

"Dick," he whispered, his eyes welling with tears, "you have to be the man of the house now."

His words hung in the air for a moment. I was twelve years old and didn't know whether to affirm their import with a nod or crouch in fear by the side of the bed. Was this Dad's way of telling me he was going to die? I looked back at him, squeezing his hand tighter. "You're going to be okay," I said, although I was thinking to myself that that probably wasn't true this time.

At the time, we didn't know much about heart disease. I just knew my father suffered from ulcers and couldn't toss the football with me in the yard as he had years before. He got winded just walking up the stairs or after doing some light housework. On this day, the pain didn't subside. Mom called for an ambulance and the paramedics rushed Dad to the hospital.

My father died eight days later. Even though I was not yet a teenager, I knew I needed to start taking responsibility for my life. I was the youngest in my family, but my two brothers, Bob and Tom, were continents away, fighting in the War. *You have to be the man of the house now.* Those words stayed in my head for the rest of my life.

Not only was I grieving the loss of my father, I also was confronted with my own mortality at a very early age. In my twenties, I began to understand the genetics of heart disease and the incredibly high probability that I would become a victim of it myself. This knowledge motivated me to lead my business and personal life in a different manner than I undoubtedly would have if I'd had no reason to doubt that a long, healthy life lay ahead of me. At one time, I was convinced that I would be dead by the age of thirty-two; and so, in my twenties, I lived every day as if that future were a looming reality. And, of course, my personal behavior became a vehicle for the realization of my worst fears: I was well on the way to creating a self-fulfilling prophecy.

At the same time, I knowingly undertook a business path that was designed to go hell-bent for leather. I was determined to "do or die," because I wasn't expecting any second chances. In retrospect, if it comes down to making a choice between career and health, I would now obviously choose my health above anything else. However—win, lose or draw—I chose the other route, and I am fortunate enough to still be kicking, or as the old Timex watch slogan goes, "Takes a licking and keeps on ticking!" And interestingly enough, my career and my health have not been strictly at odds. As my battle with heart disease unfolded, it dawned on me that my business experience offered me a unique and valuable perspective on managing my own health care. I spent virtually my entire career specializing in corporate turnarounds, taking weak and failing businesses and making them strong and profitable again. Doctors did the very same thing with my body!

Ultimately, then, the system I created combines the expertise I derived from working forty-five years in the resort and hospitality industry with the knowledge I gained in my twenty-seven years as a critical care patient. What I discovered was that the fundamentals I used to manage my companies also helped me negotiate the medical world, working through that tangled web, which is filled with its own arcane terminology and procedures.

I spent more than half my life creating and operating some of the most prestigious waterfront facilities in America. I played key roles in making the following attractions and resorts what they are today: the Balboa Bay Club, the Disneyland Hotel, the Queen Mary and the Spruce Goose, the Jockey Club, and Fisher Island in Miami. I also ran the 1984 Olympics Pentathlon competition and was a Vice President and Commissioner of the Los Angeles Summer Olympic Games. Still hard at work at age seventy-seven, I have several new projects in development. I recently sold my old company, which created and managed marinas throughout the world. I'm now chairman of Recreational Advisors International, a personal investment company I formed in 1974.

Dick receives a special welcoming committee
upon return from his first bypass.

Just as I developed hard and fast rules for overhauling companies that were hemorrhaging millions, I created similar guidelines for managing my healthcare—a system I can share with readers from the perspective of a patient, not a medical expert. You'll probably recognize some concepts in my plan. Motivational authors and business experts and advisors have addressed some of these ideas in the context of making a profit or managing personnel. The concepts are profoundly translatable: think of the profit as your health and the personnel as your own will and motivation, as well as that of the healthcare team you build.

Here is my plan, boiled down into six simple rules:

*Dick's Rules*

1. Know yourself better than your doctor does. Research what you don't know and get all the help you need to make intelligent decisions.

2. Build a team and rely on it for support. Cultivate open and positive communication with people from all walks of life.

3. Think outside the box.

4. Demand attention.

5. Develop a daily routine to enable your mental discipline.

6. Embrace persistence and *never give up*.

These concepts appear to be based on little more than common sense, but don't be fooled by their simplicity. It's all in the execution! In a sense, you're getting two books in one: insight into how my business rules saved ailing companies and a look at how my medical rules can be used to help cure ailing bodies. We'll go over each of these steps in detail in the chapters that follow. Remember as you read that, although my examples will be drawn from my personal experience with heart disease and transplantation, this plan applies to anyone who is hospitalized for a critical care emergency, whether you have cancer, diabetes, kidney disease, or any other illness. You'll find, too, that the first three steps in this plan are things you can start doing right here and now, before a hospitalization even occurs—and they may well prevent a hospitalization. However, if you do find that your condition puts you on the gurney, you'll have steps four, five, and six to carry you through.

As this book unfolds, you'll also hear from my wife, Joan, who has been my primary caretaker and support throughout the many years of my illness. Joan took the time and expended the energy and devotion to scour the internet for alternative treatments; she pestered doctors and nurses and made sure I wasn't being overlooked or overmedicated. I'm of the school of thought that if you don't have an advocate watching over your care full-time, you are at risk of becoming a victim of a terrible mistake. Joan's wisdom and watchful eye have saved my life more than once, and I asked her to join me in writing this book so that you and your caretakers can benefit from the invaluable experience she has to share.

Overall, I feel very blessed. Unlike my father, I got twenty-seven years of life (and counting!) after my first heart attack. A year after my heart transplant, I vacationed in Colorado with Joan at the wonderful Broadmoor Resort. I went hiking with the same energy I'd enjoyed during our first two years of marriage, before all my circuits blew. After I had spent the better part of two decades avoiding high altitude because it would put stress on my heart, we decided to tackle the 14,000-foot Pike's Peak. We took the train up the side of the mountain, covering more than

7,400 feet from the base to the peak during the 8.9 mile trip. There were markers every 1,000 feet in altitude, and I couldn't help but think that each one represented another hurdle in my own medical march, starting with my first heart attack in 1979. When we reached the top, I felt a little closer to my father, who never had the opportunity to make a similar journey.

"Dad," I said under my breath, "my heart feels strong. I'm alive!"

Then I turned to Joan and said, "I feel like celebrating. Let's have a cocktail!"

# Part One:
# Staying Out of the Hospital

## Chapter Two:
# Dick's First Rule:
# Know Yourself Better than
# Your Doctor Does

*"Some of the choices in life will choose you. How you face these choices, these turns in the road, with what kind of attitude, more than the choices themselves, is what will define the context of your life."*

Dana Reeve, 1961-2006

If you want to see your primary health care provider, take a good, long look in your mirror.

It's not your doctor.

It's you.

The first thing to know about your healthcare is that you're in charge of it—not your doctor, not your specialist, not your spouse. It's your responsibility to understand the state of your health in every aspect. Your doctor is simply too overworked to take on that job. He'll help you when you're sick, guide you when you need additional care, and refer you to the right specialists or institutions. But when it comes to taking charge of your healthcare, that's *your* job.

Let me show you why.

My father's death was a defining event in my life, shaping the young man I was to become. But the shockwaves of his passing went beyond the emotional and psychological: my family was faced with deep financial and practical ramifications, as well. Dad owned a successful Mercury car dealership, and until he passed away, I had led a fairly idyllic existence. But when he died, the dealership went directly to his partner, and our family was left with nothing. We had to sell our home and move into a hotel, where I shared one room with my mother. The lesson I learned, as have many others, was this: there is going to come a time—probably when you least expect it—that you will have to take responsibility for your life and what happens to you. As in a personal crisis, a health calamity can come without warning, and you may find that it's too late to take action on your own behalf. Planning ahead is a *must*.

Unfortunately, I didn't understand this lesson until many decades after Dad's death. Instead, what struck home for me was the opposite conclusion: that my health was out of my hands. Men on my father's side of the family didn't live long, and I assumed it would be no different for me. I never talked about it, but I expected to die a young man, and I made a decision to live for the moment. Translation: work hard and play every bit as hard!

As a teenager, I excelled in sports and academics, playing football in high school and college. I attended Berkeley on a track and football scholarship. I later joined the Army and served on the front lines in Korea, staying in pretty good shape throughout my twenties. After resigning from the military, I got a job in sales and my career began to take off. So did my weight. I drank liberally— three martini lunches, a bottle of wine at dinner, and a nightcap before bed. I liked pastas and beef, and pretty soon I was tipping the scale at 230, a good thirty pounds past my ideal weight. I had a penchant for working fifteen-hour days and partying long into the night with my pals and the ladies. Somehow, I survived on a few hours of sleep each night, got up, went to work, and did it all over again, day after day. I suppose my one saving grace was that I didn't smoke. What was I thinking? Well, obviously, I *wasn't* doing much, if any, thinking about my health.

Then it happened to me. At age forty-nine, I had my first heart attack. I was two years into my second marriage, and it was just a few days shy of Joan's birthday when I collapsed while walking off a tennis court after an hour of play. It happened fast. I remember feeling lightheaded and woozy before nearly fainting. Joan was walking just ahead of me when I dropped my racket and fell to one knee. When Joan heard the clatter, she knew something was wrong. She turned around, saw the helpless look on my face, and rushed to my side at once to help me to the car. I sat in the passenger seat as she got behind the wheel of our Cadillac. I leaned back and closed my eyes, and the fear that had lurked in the back of my mind all those years wrapped its icy fingers around my consciousness: *Is my number up?*

At the ER, I was seen right away. To my surprise and tremendous relief, the pain subsided, and after running a few tests, they released me that same night, seemingly none the worse for wear. The next day, I went to see a cardiologist who wasn't as reassuring. He immediately ordered an angiogram, a procedure that measures your arteries for any blockage that would restrict blood flow. Eager as ever to sidestep a confrontation with my own health, I was hoping the angiogram wouldn't interfere with my dinner plans for the evening. After all: "I'm forty-nine going on twenty, right, Doc?" But when the results arrived, I could tell from the look on my doctor's face that I'd be taking a rain check for my night out with Joan. He was brutally blunt, and I'm thankful he was. He informed me that my arteries were ninety-five percent blocked and I was at major risk for a massive myocardial infarction: in layman's terms, a fatal heart attack.

The doctor didn't mince words. "You're not leaving this hospital; you're not going home. I'm scheduling a bypass for you as soon as I can find a qualified surgical team." In the doctor's opinion, however, there were not qualified surgical teams in Orange County at that time.

A heart bypass could have saved my father, but the technology wasn't available in 1942. Dr. Michael DeBakey performed the first one in 1964, and it revolutionized heart treatment. The heart is kept alive by three major arteries that carry blood to the heart tissue. If they close, the heart muscle fed by these vessels will die, and if enough of the heart muscle dies, there's nothing to push blood to your vital organs and brain. The bypass my doctor recommended would route the blood around the blocked coronary arteries, using healthy blood vessels extracted from another part of the body—in my case, the leg. In effect, the doctor constructs a detour around the bad artery and builds a new travel pathway for the blood. Two days later, I underwent a triple bypass at St. Vincent Hospital in Los Angeles.

I had been officially diagnosed with heart disease. I would spend the next twenty-one years in and out of hospitals, racking up millions of dollars in medical bills and hundreds of lost hours from work and my family. Although my condition was hereditary, I certainly could have treated my body better with a steady regimen of exercise and improved eating habits. I had acted recklessly, certain that another miracle would save me.

After the bypass, I started to mend my ways. I double-checked my insurance plans and drew up durable powers of attorney and a medical directive. I reviewed my wills and financial arrangements, realizing I could go at any time and might not have the capacity to deal with my assets if I were lying in a hospital bed in a coma. I also started getting regular physicals and learned how to read my blood test results and medical charts. The hard part was knocking off the lasagna and New York steak dinners and sticking to a consistent exercise program. Thank goodness I didn't smoke, because that would have killed me for sure. The most crucial change I made, however, was that I finally became determined to undertake the responsibility for knowing my body better than my doctor did. I had no choice, if I wanted to live.

## Keep Tabs on Your Own Well-Being

I wish I could simply say to you, "Go ask your doctor for help," and that would be the end of this book. But do you remember your last checkup? The waiting room was probably crowded with patients, and the office help was no doubt harried. Most physicians nowadays are pressed for time, thanks to the advent of HMOs and PPOs, which limit contact between doctors and their patients. Worse yet, your best interest—getting lots of time and attention—unfortunately competes with your doctor's best interest, which often means getting through the day, seeing as many patients as possible, keeping his records and billing up-to-date, and somehow keeping up with the latest news and information about the practice of medicine. What doctor has time to do all that in a spectacular fashion? Maybe the doctors on TV medical dramas do. But all too few doctors can get that done in the real world.

Moreover, you simply cannot rely on your doctor to remember every detail from your last visit. And even if you have the best, most solicitous doctor in the world, he or she won't be a mind reader! You are the only person who has constant access to your symptoms, your feelings, and your experiences. If something feels different to you or doesn't seem to be functioning as it should, note it and *ask*. Your doctor's only mechanism for gathering information about your health is to perform tests, but he or she has no way of knowing which tests are necessary without your keen insight and input.

Here's the most important question: Do you want to live as healthy a life as possible, and are you willing to invest time, energy, and effort toward that goal? That's the bottom line.

## Take Care of Your Body and Know Your Limits

I believe that I might well have avoided many of the complications I experienced later in life if I had respected my body early on by exercising, avoiding excessive alcohol, and eating a healthy diet. Another crucial factor is simply to listen to the indications your body is giving you and to respect those limits. Here's an example, and another instance of airport medical mayhem. I was on my way to a business appointment in Vancouver, B.C., and only as my plane was landing in Seattle to clear customs did I discover that I had left my passport at home. However, one of the airline attendants told me that if I rushed to the customs office between planes, I could get a temporary passport. So, as soon as we landed, I started running through the terminal, hoping to get a passport and still catch my connecting flight. It seemed like the perfect plan—until I started down an escalator, passed out cold, and tumbled down the moving stairs, taking out several people as I fell. (Fortunately, none of them was seriously injured.) I was left with some new creases in my skull from the metal corrugated escalator steps, along with a pretty badly banged-up head and body.

When I awoke, I was looking into the faces of some paramedics who were doing their best to revive me. My internal defibrillator was still going off, shocking my heart back into action. Although I was taken to a local hospital, it was the shocks from the defibrillator that saved me. I was able to fly home the next morning.

The lesson here is that there is no possible reason you should push your body beyond its logical constraints, no point in "testing fate." There is no meeting important enough to place yourself at risk of losing everything. Be smart—or smarter than I was.

Once you do know your limits, trust yourself. You might find that even qualified medical personnel are suggesting that you go beyond your body's current capabilities. But know that just because a person works in the medical profession doesn't mean you have to accept his or her advice at face value, especially if it goes against your instincts. People are human. On one occasion, I was seriously hurt by acting on the advice of a physical therapist.

The therapist had me doing sit-ups when I had just come out of the hospital with my stomach and chest all torn up. I thought it was strange, but I didn't say anything. That was a mistake. Several hernias resulted, which are still with me.

So, what did I do wrong? My instincts told me sit-ups didn't make sense, but I didn't question the therapist. Always question your caregivers, therapists, nurses, and doctors if you don't understand why they are making a recommendation. Always. Sometimes the personnel assigned to you have great knowledge of the workout, medication, or other treatment they may be administering, but they don't always have a thorough understanding of the medical ramifications that you may experience. You must be your own advocate. Don't be shy or worried about offending someone when it comes to making sure what's taking place is truly in your best interest.

## Check Your Hormone Levels

Checking your hormone levels is just as important as checking the oil in your car. Most people operate unaware of their hormones, but hormones, or lack thereof can be the cause of certain illnesses. Consider having your hormones analyzed. This is true whether you are a woman or a man. New research demonstrates that aging men with lower testosterone levels are at an increased risk for prostate cancer. Whereas, replacement testosterone therapy used to be thought of as increasing one's risk for prostate cancer, this new research disproves this theory and encourages hormone therapy. For detailed findings and further explanation on testosterone replacement see, Harvard-based Dr. Abraham Morgentaler's book, *Testosterone for Life*.

When older people get sick, it's often a hormone deficiency or a result of unbalanced hormones. So have your levels checked annually, or more often if you are unwell. We have used natural hormones—compounded at a compounding pharmacy—for many years. There is no risk to one's health with such treatment. Joan found Suzanne Somers' book, *Ageless: The Naked Truth about Bio-identical Hormones* extremely helpful and we recommend it as an introduction for the lay reader to the concept of hormone therapy.

You can read more on this important subject in Appendix One, An Interview with Dr. Cooke. In *The Sexy Years: Discover the Hormone Connection*, Suzanne Somers writes extensively about hormones and our bodies need for them. Christine Northrup's *Women's Bodies, Women's Wisdom: Creating Physical and Emotional Health and Healing* is another great source. Keep in mind that this attention to hormones is not just for women. It is an equally vital area of concern for men and absolutely essentially for maintaining good health. Dr. Cooke's interview goes into more detail about this important, but often overlooked, area of our health plan.

## Keep Your Checkup Appointments

Your doctors can't help you if they don't see you regularly. We're used to thinking of a checkup as a yearly affair, but your doctor may recommend more frequent visits as you age or if you become afflicted with illness. You may also need to check in regularly with different specialists rather than only with your generalist. There is simply no way to overestimate the importance of these appointments—in fact, a routine checkup was what saved me from more colon cancer. I had just returned home from a vacation and was feeling pretty good when I went to USC for a normal, quarterly checkup. I was with my surgeon, Dr. Mark Barr, when the lab called him with the results of my blood work and other tests. The doctor almost fainted. I had lost a huge amount of blood—but where, and how?

I was rushed to Hoag Hospital and slapped into a bed, "stat." Then began a three-day search for the source of the bleeding. My internist thought it was probably an ulcer, but they simply couldn't detect it, let alone pinpoint its location. Finally, they located the spot in my colon, near the Ileo-Cecal (IC) valve. A young surgeon was able to go in arthroscopically and remove the lesion, along with about a foot of my colon. The biopsy revealed that the cells were malignant. They tested all the lymph glands in the area, and thankfully, those were clean. Since I was diligently keeping my regular and frequent checkup appointments, we caught my cancer early and nipped it in the bud. As they say, "an ounce of prevention is worth a pound of cure." The take-home point in this instance? Take the time or *make* the time for complete and frequent checkups.

## Keep Up-to-Date Documents on Hand

The buck doesn't stop with your immediate physical condition. You've also got to understand the practical, legal, and financial ramifications of your potential illness and take steps to prepare. Your doctor and your caretakers, including your closest family members, need to have a way of accessing information about your health. If this information is only stored away in the back of your mind or in a file drawer that no one knows about but you, it could mean catastrophe. Here's a checklist of five crucial items that are in your control *at this moment:*

1. Create a list of the medications you take and any critical care needs you might have, and keep it on your person *at all times*. Put it in your wallet or purse, and give a copy to your spouse or partner. Update it every time your doctor adds a medication or changes a dosage. Being aware of your own medication list and making this information readily available to your caretakers and doctors is so crucial that I'll devote an entire section to it below. But first, let's look at the remaining four crucial documents.

2. List your key doctors and other contacts for medical care, their specialties, and their phone numbers. This list should be kept at home, in your emergency folder, which should be accessible to your spouse, family members, and anyone else who might be called upon on short notice to help in your survival. It also doesn't hurt to keep a copy of this list on your person.

3. List the people (family members, friends, doctors, specialists) who should be notified in the event of your hospitalization and any messages or instructions these people should receive. Keep this list in your emergency folder at home and on your person.

4. Create a will and keep it current. I'm willing to bet that 50 percent of my readers either don't have a will or have an outdated one. A current will is absolutely essential to whoever handles your affairs if you find yourself in the hospital without warning.

5. Create a power of attorney and a durable power of attorney for health and medical care (the name varies from state to state). The latter document will allow your next of kin, or

whomever you designate, to make medical decisions on your behalf if you are unable to do so yourself.

## Inventory Your Medications

I really want to stress how critical it is that every patient carefully review and record the names of their medications—both prescribed and over-the-counter—the condition each medication treats, and the proper dosage of each medication. This list also should contain any information about allergic reactions you might have to any type of medication or treatment. Be sure to date the list so that you and your doctors can quickly tell how current it is. Joan and I recommend that you make sure at least two or three members of your team (which includes your spouse/significant other, friends and family members, doctors and health support staff) also have updated copies readily available.

In far too many cases, I have seen that individuals, both pre- and post-operation, have neglected to keep their drug list up-to-date because it seems like a laborious task. However, the short amount of time you spend doing this is a small price to pay in exchange for the life-saving tool a med list will be in your doctors' hands. If you are in an accident or have a critical care emergency, your doctors will rely heavily on whatever information they can find on you to head off giving you a contraindicated medication, or over- or under-dosing you. Even if you are awake and calm, it's not always an easy task to remember the complicated names of medications and exactly what they were prescribed for. Keep your list handy even for non-emergency appointments with your doctor.

Here's a story from Joan about how absolutely vital it is to make sure that you aren't the only person with a copy of your med list:

> Dick was once taken into the ER at Hoag Hospital in Newport Beach because of a cluster of blood clots that had developed in his groin. Until this particular incident, Dick had always remembered his drugs, and he always had a copy of his med list. I never kept a copy of my own. When the paramedics came, Dick was wearing shorts and didn't have his wallet, with the list in it, on him. By the time we reached the ER, they were giving him morphine and more morphine, and they still couldn't get rid of the pain. Naturally, in that state, Dick couldn't remember very much or very clearly—certainly not enough to list the roughly thirty different medications he was taking at that point. Even with all of the experiences we'd already had prior to this one, I didn't have a current copy of his meds with me. I felt like a moron. The doctors had no way of knowing that they were treating him properly.

Keeping abreast of your own records can extend beyond medication, as well. For example, when I "died" at the airport in San Diego, a doctor wanted to run several tests that would have put incredible stress on my body. Joan intervened and put a stop to the test order because she was aware that I had undergone the same battery of tests just twelve months earlier in Arizona. Joan put the San Diego doctors in touch with the hospital in Phoenix to get copies of the records, saving my body needless stress and danger. This is just one example of how valuable it can be to remain vigilant about your own medical history.

## Do Your Homework

In all my years of dealing with surgeons and hospitals, I've learned that there's no substitute for doing your own homework. When you don't know the answer yourself, you can almost always find a resource that will give you the answer, whether this means unabashedly quizzing your nurses and doctors or combing through the internet to gather background on your surgeon, data on the latest treatments, or federal ratings on everything from hospital infection rates to the frequency of transplants performed. In the Reference section toward the back of this book, you'll find links to significant websites with data and studies that show, for example, which areas of the country have the shortest and longest waits for new organs. You'll also find a detailed checklist so that you can measure how ready you are for a catastrophic illness.

If you're setting out to know yourself better than your doctor does, you're going to need a little help. You might feel like you're back in high school again, gathering sources for that term paper. But if you truly care about taking control of your own healthcare, this won't be a chore. Your body is a fascinating and wonderful machine. I guarantee that, the more you discover, the more eager you'll be to learn more. And the more you know, the more empowered you'll be to make the best possible decisions you can for your own well-being. The medical system doesn't have to seem foreign and overwhelming. If you can learn to work alongside it, you'll reap enormous rewards.

# Chapter Three:
# Dick's Second Rule:
# Build a Team and Cultivate
# Communication

I'm not sure I'd be alive today if I didn't treat my medical team as extended family. In many ways, I was fortunate to have learned the importance of opening up and cultivating new relationships and support teams at a young age. From bonding with others, from my high school football coaches and teammates to my college fraternity brothers to my military buddies, I've come to believe you can find family almost anywhere, if you're open to it. When I entered the business world, team-building became a core fundamental of my management philosophy, whether is was part of a reorganization, a startup or a takeover. And—surprise! This stood me in good stead in my battle with heart disease. As in almost any other area of life, I found that the one-man band, the person who tries to run everything by himself, usually will fail.

The tie between business and healthcare is pretty obvious: if you neglect to delegate work outside your area of expertise and undertake tasks that easily could be handled by someone else, you're taking a risk. Better to focus your energies on what's important and central to the objective. One of my best examples of team building was the group I put together over a weekend to win the Balboa Bay Club contract years ago. I had an idea to develop a waterfront apartment complex at a prominent private club in Newport Beach, California. After six months of networking, calls, and letters, I got an appointment with my future mentor, Jack Wrather. Jack was an oil tycoon who founded the Disneyland Hotel. Experience had taught me to reach out to one of his associates before my appointment with him, and this was how I learned he was a no-nonsense leader; it was imperative to be prepared when you walked through his door, or you would most surely fail. The problem was, I knew nothing about clubs, hotels, or food and beverage! Over a weekend, I scrambled to create a team of architects and an interior designer, and I developed some drawings and models. I presented my plan to Mr. Wrather during a brief Monday meeting. I won the job, but not because I was a terrific interior designer or architect. I left those tasks to people who could make me look good. In effect, I started at the top because I was able to organize a team of people who knew their business. This relationship lasted more than twenty years. Whether it's in business or in health, it pays to identify what you *don't* know and to find the proper help in those areas, delegating those tasks while you concentrate on what you do best.

This life skill became invaluable to me when I began to face increasingly serious medical crises. When you're confronted with the possibility of spending weeks or months in the hospital, you can't go it alone. The good news is that team building is something you can start right now, ideally before you even set foot in the hospital. Begin by nurturing a medical network that includes your family doctor, specialists, surgeons, therapists, nurses, technicians, rehabilitation workers/physical therapists, and the hospital support staff. Keep open lines of communication with these individuals, and if you can, facilitate their communication with each other about your case. Your team, of course, will extend far beyond the medical profession. Begin to talk with your friends and family about your condition and ensure that you can rely on their support both emotionally and for your day-in and day-out needs.

The next step, which is a skill I believe all people should cultivate—whether or not they are facing a hospital stay—is to learn to communicate openly and empathetically with people from all walks of life. People in support roles, such as nurses and even hospital custodians, will ultimately have a tremendous amount of power over your comfort and contact with your physicians. You'll see them constantly, while you'll see your doctor only a few minutes a day, at best. You'll be relying on them for both your care and well-being as they assist you in performing the day-to-day functions you once did for yourself. Don't overlook these individuals. Instead, seek to establish genuine relationships with them.

The key here, as with all good, healthy relationships, is communication. Treat all of these wonderful people like brothers or sisters; ask them about their lives, how they're doing, how their families are. If you can stand out as the one patient who recognizes the hard work they do rather than bombarding them with a litany of complaints, you'll find your kindness returned manifold. On the other hand, if you are the grouch that all the nurses want to avoid, do you think you'll get a swift response when you push the call button at two a.m.? The quality of your care is ultimately in your own hands. You get back what you put out.

This kind of open and genuine communication is a fundamental trait of all successful leaders. These skills can inspire a workforce and customer base. When I took over the world-famous Miami resort, Fisher Island, my first priority was reinvigorating the blasé workforce. I created a contest and named it, "If I Were President." The concept was to encourage the employees to submit ideas to improve the operation. I rewarded the best proposals with cash prizes—always a great motivator! Not only did I get some great ideas, but staff morale improved as well. They appreciated that someone cared enough to listen to their opinions.

By the same token, each time I was hospitalized, I made sure I knew everyone's name who worked around and with me. I asked them about their families and their background, treating everyone with the same respect. It's just a fact that people will bend over backwards for you when you show a little interest and kindness to them as individuals. I cannot overstress the necessity of establishing productive relationships with the medical staff, just the same as you would want to do in a relationship with an employee, colleague, or client. You've got to convince them you are worthy of extra care and attention because, let me tell you, in the hospital and healthcare systems, you are most definitely bargaining for their precious time—and your life may depend upon it.

I'll share with you another of my medical adventures that illustrates how vital my support network was for me. In August of 2006, six years after my heart transplant, I was a much healthier man. My not-so-new heart was pumping vigorously, and in preparation for relaxing a bit more with Joan, I had recently sold several of my companies and started working on my book. But my routine was interrupted one evening after dinner when I went upstairs to my office to get some papers from my desk. As I was reaching for the file cabinet, my legs suddenly felt like they were splitting open; it was as though I had been shot in both legs. This caused the most unimaginable pain, and I fell to the floor screaming; in fact, I lost my voice after a few moments, because the pain was so acute. As Joan rushed upstairs, I lay where I had fallen, trapped between my desk and the file cabinet. Joan frantically dialed 911; the paramedics, bless them, arrived in three minutes flat.

"We can't do anything with him here," I heard a paramedic tell Joan as they placed me on a gurney. I thought to myself, "Here we go again." We rushed to Hoag Hospital, just a few minutes' drive from our house. The ER doctors diagnosed that a number of blood clots had broken loose in my groin area, creating a virtual 4th of July fireworks explosion there. Still, there was one blessing in all of this: had the clots flowed in the other direction, toward my heart, I would have suffered a massive heart attack or stroke. The Hoag doctors said I needed surgery at once or I would lose my legs—yes, lose them, as in amputation.

Joan was panicked about my condition, but she was equally concerned about how we would possibly find a qualified surgical team to help me late on a Friday night in August. She called Dr. Mark Barr, my heart transplant surgeon, and Dr. Virginia Cooke, a former vascular surgeon who tired to line up surgeons at UCLA while helping doctors at Hoag. The Hoag doctors also made calls. Joan asked all of them to try to form surgical teams, and whoever got to the finish line first got the job. It turned out that Barr and a team he found at USC won that race, and I was flown by helicopter to downtown Los Angeles—reducing what would have been an hour-plus drive to a mere ten minutes.

Dr. Fred Weaver is the talented surgeon who performed the procedure. I've included a fascinating interview with him in the Appendix at the end of this book. It was thanks to our relationship with Dr. Barr that we connected with Dr. Weaver.

So, what did I learn this time around?

1. The necessity of having medical experts at your call to help form your medical team, whatever or whenever the crisis occurs.

2. The importance of having a patient advocate close by—in this case, my wife Joan—to help troubleshoot, monitor medication intake, check technical procedures, and provide basic help.

Joan has been simply superhuman in her role as caregiver. But it was paramount that, even as I was undergoing years of treatment and recurring crises, Joan was able to not only provide for my care, but take time for herself as well. If you find yourself in an acute medical situation, you must be able to rely fully and unabashedly on the friends and family members whom you've selected as your caregivers. At the same time, in order to make this leap of faith, you must feel confident that your caregivers have a system in place for *their own care*. Many of you reading this book no doubt find yourself in the role of caregiver. In many cases, the family caregiver is either a spouse or the adult child who lives closest to the parent(s) needing care.

Joan and I decided that staying in a nursing home, long term, was not an option for me. I am so grateful that we made that decision. If possible, you want to keep yourself or a loved one out of a nursing home when recovering from a serious illness. When you go on a tour, nursing homes, especially in affluent areas, look great. The facilities are often beautiful and the staff seems to be highly professional and attentive. But the reality of day-to-day life in a nursing home can be miserable and depressing ... and even fatal.

Nurses or attendants may deliver medication to the bedside of the patient, but do they actually stay there and make sure the patient takes the medication? All too often, the answer is no. How do they know the patient is taking the medication and not simply dropping it on the floor? The same thing is true with meals: is the patient eating what he or she is supposed to eat, or does the meal go untouched? What about a patient who cannot transfer to the bathroom without assistance? It can take forever for an attendant or nurse to get to the patient and help them get to the bathroom. If the specter of your loved one, or yourself, lying in a pool of urine in bed isn't enough to keep you from buying into the concept of a nursing home, I don't know what will.

Nursing homes are absolutely not an option for patients in need of constant care. They are suitable when you are recovering from a knee injury or hip replacement and require physical therapy. I know people who have received good care in nursing homes when recovering from these types of surgeries.

According to some recent U.S. statistics, one quarter of adults are presently providing care for an aging parent or relative, with nearly half that number are caring for their spouse. Even though caregiving for family members is often rewarding in many ways, it can also most assuredly be stressful, potentially causing tension within families. Furthermore, a lot of this stress is quietly absorbed by the caregiver, who feels guilty if they talk about it, let alone do anything proactive about it. A recent study by a prominent senior care organization revealed that 31 percent of family caregivers admit they'd like more help, with 25 percent reporting their resentment of other family members who don't pitch in and help out more.

The stress of caregiving can also be compounded if the caregiver has other pressing responsibilities, such as a job, children to care for, social obligations, distance to travel to provide the care, and so on. Caregiving can be especially difficult for a spouse when the care recipient requires assistance 24/7. This leads to an increased potential for danger to the spousal caregiver if they have or develop their own health issues to contend with; these health problems all too often are exacerbated, not just by the stress itself, but by the typical decision to ignore or put off giving attention to their own needs.

Caregivers who take care of themselves in *body, mind, and soul* will ultimately have more physical and emotional stamina and peace of mind, which will create a balance that allows them to take better care of their loved ones. You may want to begin your day with a meditation period. In pragmatic terms, meditation simply means taking enough oxygen into the deepest part of your lungs to strengthen your entire immune system.

Meditation allows the brain to settle down into a more comfortable pattern, taking away all the jarring thoughts that we live with day and night when caring for another. When I was in dire shape at the hospital, Joan would begin her day with a twenty-minute meditation tape, just to get centered. Neither she nor I can recommend meditation enough. Here, Joan will share some of the techniques she discovered during the many years that she found herself in the caregiver and advocate role for me:

> Caregivers simply *must* find ways to take care of themselves. You may try to rationalize that you don't have a lot of time or that your needs aren't as urgent. But the bottom line is, if you can't keep yourself as strong and healthy as possible, how in the world can you expect the patient to keep going? People often asked me, "How can you look at what goes on there? How do you keep going?" My answer was that I would walk down that Intensive Care Unit (ICU) hallway, see all the other people there, and I would always notice that there was somebody who had something worse going on. The truth of the matter is that it can always get worse, so I would never allow myself to think negatively. I'd be sure to focus on the positive outcome, one day at a time, not just with the big picture.

> I developed several habits to take care of my body and soothe my mind during the many times Dick was in the hospital. I began practicing yoga; I used 20-minute meditation tapes; I went to the gym three days a week to work out with a trainer; I got my nails done every couple of weeks; and I got massages whenever possible. I gave myself permission to rest in the evening instead of answering phone calls; I knew that the people who loved me would understand. I discovered Red Bull to keep me awake on the long drives home from the hospital! I took B-100 vitamin complex, which is a great stress reliever. And we followed Norman Cousins' lead and

laughed as much as possible. Laughter has so many healing properties and is a great way of releasing endorphins; it's therapeutic for the caregiver and the patient. While Dick was in the hospital, we'd watch about fifteen comedy movies a week. I can't emphasize enough how important it is to always think positively. When I think about how so many people are given terrible prognoses, I wish more people wouldn't just throw in the towel and give up. I've seen amazing miracles; they're not as rare as you might think.

I want to share my experience during the time Dick "died" at the airport in San Diego. While Dick was in the airport, I was at a seminar on guided imagery with our daughter Lisa. During an exercise at the seminar, one of the therapists asked me to visualize: "You can visualize a rose or anything way you want." As soon as the rose came into my mind, I started crying hysterically—and I'm not a big crier. The therapist asked me, "What do you think you're crying about?" There was nothing wrong with Dick at this time; he was in really good shape, and he had just gone to Mexico. But I said, "Well, the only thing I can think of is, my husband has a heart condition, and I just don't want the rose to die." We realized later that Dick collapsed in the airport at the exact moment that I got so emotional about not wanting the rose to die.

My daughter Sandy also has been one of my major caregivers. Here is her advice:

During the many crises that Dad has endured, I feel very fortunate that I was able to rely on a support system of friends and family. They started to call me "Mother Control Central." Whenever there was new information about Dad, I would call one friend, who would then call five other people in our support system and keep the information rolling.

I think I know a thousand ways to sit in a hospital chair. I found all kinds of ways to occupy my time in the hospital so it didn't seem so endless. I would suggest taking a variety of things to pass the time: books, music, puzzles, things to keep your mind occupied. Many hospitals are pretty sterile—you only have a TV, and I found myself mindlessly trying to read the same paragraph over and over again in a book. Then I started doing more journal work, writing things down, and that helped. I also tried to interact with other people and find out what was going on with them.

It's important for the family to know their blood type so they can donate to family members going through these kinds of ordeals. It gives you something to do when you're waiting, to go and donate, and you feel like you're doing something really helpful.

Dad had such a long wait to receive his heart. I learned from that experience how to figure out ways to avoid heavy traffic in any way possible. I encourage anyone who has a long commute to go visit their loved one in the hospital or long-term care to stay aware of alternate travel routes in case the freeway is jammed; map them out for yourself and drive them a few times, so you're familiar with them. Listen to the radio, stay apprised of traffic and just stay very aware and alert while making those long treks.

During long vigils, especially, I encourage people to do whatever makes them feel best so they can keep going. I remember going to breakfast with Joan once. It was early into one of Dad's surgeries, and I said, "I'm sorry, Mom, but I'm going to have a glass of wine and a hamburger at 6:00 in the morning, so I can put myself to sleep!"

Friends are really important during these situations. There is no better care than you will find in friends. Our dear friend, Kara Fox, drove for many miles, day and night, just to be with Joan. It was very comforting for Joan and a wonderful feeling for me to know that someone was with her when she really needed it. When you go through one of these situations, you really find out how wonderful people can be.

The emotional and physical burden of taking care of a loved one with a serious illness or disease is enormous. Sometimes, it's just physically impossible for a smaller person to help a heavier person move from the bed to the bathroom! Combine the physical challenge with the emotional challenge of watching a loved one suffer or decline, and it's a setup for depression and serious illness. Again, the caretaker must take great care of herself or himself, or risk illness or even death. This isn't anecdotal; this is a proven fact.

For those of you who have a wife or companion with a catastrophic illness, caregiving can become the most satisfying experiences of your life. That sounds strange, given all the heartache and stress involved in a loved one's hospitalization, but Joan and I have reached a new level in our 31-year long marriage. You, too, can find greater joy in your relationship. Part of it comes from facing the prognosis that you might not be around much longer, and part of it comes from the appreciation of having a spouse who is dedicated to your well-being and your survival.

I wonder at all the things we have accomplished as a couple, and I wonder at all the things that Joan has done by herself. She truly is a magnificent woman. I wonder at how she has held us together through thick and thin (boy, were some days thin!) and evolved into a loving, thoughtful friend and companion. During the past twenty-nine years, she has been by my side through my various health problems. This is no small testimonial in itself, but in the meantime, through study and experience, she has become a bit of a medical expert herself—so much so that a great number of her friends consult her when they are worried about a medical or personal problem. She is always there for them. I am so proud of her, and that has added to the love affair we have.

Our love affair has never been as wonderful as it is now, and I enjoy and appreciate every minute I have with her. God has been with her and all the many men and women who find themselves in similar circumstances. Do not despair. Look at your medical challenges as an opportunity to experience the love of your life. We did.

# Chapter Four:
# Dick's Third Rule:
# Think Outside the Box

I am convinced that a large part of the reason I'm alive today is that Joan and I adopted some unconventional therapies to treat my illness—while still following my doctors' orders. I have friends, like investor Peter Rothschild, who shared my philosophy during their own medical ordeals and took charge of their bodies and medical care, with great results. I have two friends who contracted cancer. One took chances, tried alternative therapies, and listened to doctors with fresh approaches; twenty-five years later, he's still alive. Another fine man, my mentor, Jack Wrather, about whom I shared a bit in the previous chapter, chose to stick with the conventional doctors and treatments. Unfortunately, he died after a few short years.

While I am extremely thankful for all the caring, wonderful medical professionals I have met and worked with along this journey of mine, I am also grateful that my wife Joan and I have done our best to keep our hearts and minds open to some alternative modalities of healing. I hope you'll read the following with an open heart and mind, as we have written it. If you find truth or comfort in it, that's great! On the other hand, perhaps it will simply provide some food for thought. For us, some of the things I'll describe in this chapter have done both. We don't include these ideas in an effort to convert anyone to our way of thinking or believing. But our belief system is such an integral part of how we've lived our lives and dealt with my many health crises that I feel it merits examination and hopefully will stimulate some interesting discussion, even if it's just with yourself. It's all good!

In business, I spent my professional lifetime thinking outside the box. During the Korean War, I was assigned to Japan for several years, and I had control of a huge amount of electronic supplies. I was only in my early twenties at the time; you might say I was the Sergeant Bilko of the Far East. I swung deals for hard-to-get facilities and electronic equipment for my troops by swapping high demand sports gear—baseball bats and footballs I accumulated in the off-seasons—all by the rules. I traded what I had for specialized work to furnish my troops with better living conditions and recreational facilities.

Years later, I helped raise $100 million for Hughes Aircraft by transforming three high-rise apartment buildings built on county land into hybrid condominiums. I put the *Spruce Goose*—Howard Hughes's classic airplane—and the great ocean liner *The Queen Mary* side by side, developing them into one of

California's top tourist attractions and saving that historic plane from destruction. I did all this by always thinking outside the box and giving the contrarian viewpoint a chance, which many times led to the achievement of things that were previously considered impossible.

I want to share with you several examples of how I applied my "outside the box" thinking to my healthcare. Hopefully, this will get your creative juices flowing, too.

## An Alternative to Mainstream Shortfalls

With the conclave of wildly popular movies, television shows and books that have cropped up over the past twenty years such as *Ghost, The Sixth Sense,* television's *Touched By An Angel,* Lisa Williams's *Life Among the Dead, Medium,* and *Ghost Whisperer*—along with bestselling books by authors Doreen Virtue, Jerry and Esther Hicks, John Holland, and many others—it's obvious Joan and I are far from being alone in our beliefs. Maybe, just maybe, there's more than the naked eye can see at work on this old Earth, and perhaps much help can be derived from these sources, if we're willing to ask. Allow me to give you some very logical statistics to consider and bear in mind:

1. The respected Institute of Medicine in Washington, D.C. conducted a study on the risks of medication errors and reported in July, 2006 that more than 1.5 million Americans are killed and injured each year by medication mistakes. The cost is in the billions. The study further reported that there are 400,000 preventable drug-related injuries that take place in hospitals annually, costing at least $3.5 billion.

The Spruce Goose, the world's largest airplane, moves
into its new home in Long Beach, California.

2. In August, 2006, the *Los Angeles Times* ran an article that reported that the state Medi-Cal program notified four organ-transplant programs that they could lose their state funding because they have excessive patient deaths or perform too few surgeries. In all, since 2005, seven California hospitals have been cited by federal and state officials for failing to perform the minimum number of organ transplants for state and federal certification and funding.

3. The *San Francisco Chronicle* revealed in May of 2006 that Kaiser Permanente San Francisco had to move 2,000 kidney patients from its waitlist to transplant programs elsewhere after federal officials learned that twice as many people died on the waitlist than those who actually received kidneys in 2005. The ratio is supposed to be exactly the opposite.

It's an unfortunate fact that there are countless similar horror stories. Throughout this book, we have made it our mission to do our best to share with you the best ways we've discovered to avoid unnecessary pitfalls and pain when it comes to hospital stays and your health care. Perhaps, once you have absorbed and mulled over the errors that pervade our medical expertise in this country, you also might find yourself more open to the idea of seeking out some unconventional energy healing, or at least remaining open to the possibility that we still have a long way to go with our conventional medical treatment. Remember, it's a good idea to assemble a powerful arsenal of resources, no matter how unconventional you might think them to be at first. There's a lot to that old adage that the best offense is a good defense. Surgery should be the last option.

Do not reject nor refuse assistance, as long as you believe it may, indeed, serve your Highest Good. Other cultures have practiced healing rituals for many centuries. Asian cultures have practiced acupuncture for many hundreds of years, and we are just learning how to use it for our benefit in the U.S. When I found myself dealing with heart failure and waiting for my transplant, I discovered I was not (and still am not) prepared to discount anything which might remotely be helpful to me. How about you?

## The Miracle of CoQ10

Just by reading through the brief synopsis of my business background in Chapter One, you can see that, long before I had heart problems, I grasped the concept that risk could reap rewards. When Joan showed me an article about the amazing effects on the heart from the over-the-counter supplement known as coenzyme Q10 (CoQ10), I was willing to listen, even though my cardiologist was unfamiliar at the time with the benefits of the enzyme. It was 1995, and I had just suffered another heart attack. My heart was so weak that doctors inserted a defibrillator in my body to shock my heart back into rhythm when it ran out of gas. When the defibrillator went off, the jolt was so violent it would knock me out of my chair. My doctors put me on a waitlist for a heart transplant, warning that I might not last the year without one. Luckily, I lasted six years, and I'm convinced CoQ10 had something to do with it.

Here is Joan's story of how she discovered CoQ10:

> I first found out about CoQ10 back in the early 1990s, when we were living in Arizona. Dick had already been evaluated in Tucson for a heart transplant; they told him that he would need one inside of a year. Our daughter Lisa happened to be visiting us from Mexico at the time, and

one day she and I went to the health food store. They tend to put lots of informative brochures and magazines in your bags; while I was unloading the groceries, my daughter was reading one of these magazines and came upon this big article about CoQ10. We had not heard of it in those days, but she got very excited when she read what the Texas cardiologist who was interviewed in the article had to say about it, so she gave it to me.

This cardiologist had been administering CoQ10 to a woman on a transplant list there, and by the time the article was printed, it had been thirteen years, she still hadn't needed a transplant—amazing! I immediately called this cardiologist, told him Dick's situation, and asked him what he thought. He said, "Oh, yeah! Put him on it."

So we went back to the health food store, bought the highest dosage available, which I believe at that time was 100 milligrams, and we put Dick on it. Within five days, we could see the difference. There are no side effects of CoQ10. As time went on, and Dick would start failing again, I would double the dose, and he would come right back up—every single time. We asked all of our doctors in L.A. and Arizona about it, and they all said, "Well, we've never heard of it, but from what it says, it's not gonna hurt him, so do whatever you want."

By the time Dick got his new heart, six years later, he was taking 600 milligrams a day. We've recommended it to several people we know with heart problems since then, and they've all seen great results. If you really have heart failure and problems along those lines, the results you'll witness will very likely be dramatic. We are not suggesting you follow the regimen we chose; you need to do some due diligence, research it, get advice from anyone you trust, and then make your own decision about whether and how to use it. Over the past few years, we've seen this wonder supplement go from unknown status to becoming a bit of a "rock star" in the world of heart care. It's now very commonly recommended by hospitals and leading cardiologists.

In a 2006 study in Italy, researchers reported that the heart tissue contains the highest concentration of CoQ10 in the human body. They found evidence that plasma CoQ10 levels decrease in patients with advanced chronic heart failure. Consequently, daily oral supplements of CoQ10 improved the cardiovascular health of people with heart failure.

While the majority of research has focused on CoQ10's pivotal role in cardiovascular health, the scope of its healing properties is steadily widening, with studies emerging that show it also provides benefits to people suffering from diabetes, cancer (breast, lung and prostate), male infertility, and kidney failure.

## Healers

While I was on the transplant list, a number of our friends offered to help in a myriad of ways. One friend of ours had a long-standing association with a wonderful gentleman from the African nation of Senegal. He was a healer as well as a major political leader there, and came from a politically strong family. He had generated a legion of followers worldwide who swore by his ability to heal. He had groups in New York as well as California who were diligent disciples and witnesses of his methods and gifts.

Our friend was convinced this man had some kind of mystical power and believed it would be worthwhile for us to have a visit with him. Joan and I were quite surprised, to say the least, when this ebony-skinned fellow arrived on our doorstep in Newport Beach, decked out in full, flowing native robes, accompanied by an interpreter in similar garb. The healer spoke not a word of English, only French. As I took it all in, I couldn't help thinking to myself, "What in the world am I doing? Putting it mildly, this is pretty far removed from any hospital-approved regimen I've ever come across!"

Still, we felt privileged to spend some time with this beautiful soul; he actually visited us on several occasions. He would do such highly religious acts as to blow on me (yes, blow his breath upon me), which was done to convey blessings to me. He also gave me a slip of paper with a phrase in his native tongue written upon it; I was instructed to memorize this and to repeat it to myself as I was going into the operating room. While I certainly was not sold on his ability to heal me, I had decided to leave no stone unturned, no possibility untried during the many months I waited for my heart. I kept the slip of paper with me that entire time, although somehow, I misplaced it as I was preparing for surgery. I like to think that by having it close to me as long as I did, much of its healing effect rubbed off on me by osmosis, anyway! You never know. Keep your mind open.

## "There are more things in Heaven and Earth, Horatio ..."

Although I know this is likely to spark much skepticism and excessive eyebrow-raising in certain quarters, it is a part of my story, so I feel compelled to share at least an overview of it with you here. Joan and I have been longstanding advocates of the assistance provided to those on the earth plane by unseen sources such as paranormal pathways, other dimensions, and angels. Now, before you think we're going totally "Twilight-Zoney" on you, just let me remind you that we're in pretty darned good company in our willingness to give credit to this sector. Shakespeare, Sir Arthur Conan Doyle, Mark Twain, Harry Houdini, Horace Greeley, and Norwegian painter Edvard Munch are just a handful of thinkers and artists who have kept an open mind where this topic is concerned.

Personally, we've tried table-tipping over a period of twelve years. We have sought out the counsel of a very accurate medical intuitive. We have found great benefit with acupuncture treatment, and I have received some very helpful energy healing treatments, from Reiki on down the line. This is a course of action that may not be for everyone, but it has done well for us. We list several reading sources in the Bibliography.

Table-tipping is done within a protected energy circle where higher energies (guides, master teachers, and angels) communicate directly with you through table movement and telepathy. Everyone who is participating in the session receives information. We have done this for many years with Valynda Dupre and John Petri in Scottsdale, Arizona.

Our results have been outstanding. For anyone interested in knowing more about this phenomenon, we recommend reading *The Key to Spiritual and Psychic Development: Table Tipping* by Angela Mattey. It can provide a different dimension to your health program.

I suppose this is as good a time as any to tell you that I believe in guardian angels, or in a spiritual presence human beings cannot fully understand. So many things that are otherwise unexplained have happened to me. I take great comfort in feeling that there's somebody out there looking after me. Believe it or not—but keep your mind open to whatever happens to you.

One night when I was in the hospital waiting for my heart (day after day, minute after minute), I was hit at about two or three in the morning with my defibrillator going off, which was an indication that my heart had stopped or was not working properly. Of course, I was hooked up to machines that monitored all of my vital signs down at the nurse's station. It was a good, healthy kick, and I awoke with a start. The room was dark, and I knew I was not in immediate danger because the defibrillator only hit me with one jolt—which was enough. As I lay there recovering, all of a sudden the room was filled with individuals. It was still dark, and all I saw was a group of perhaps seven to ten people in the room. No one turned the lights on and no one said anything. As I turned, the nurse was at my side. All I kept saying was, "I'm all right, I'm okay," and that was it. These other figures remained silent and stayed in the room,; after a couple of minutes, they all left.

It didn't strike me as unusual until I thought about it the next day. At that time of night on my floor in the ICU, there were only one or two nurses on duty. The place was as quiet as a church, as you might expect it to be. It suddenly hit me that perhaps the angels had come to collect my weary body and take me to Heaven, or wherever. They never said anything, and neither did I, and all was well. One can imagine that it was a hallucination on my part, or that some emergency people came from out of nowhere, but the absence of conversation and/or action on their part indicated otherwise. Now, I don't know if this means anything or not, but it strikes me as extremely unusual and again underscores the need for someone in critical care to be aware of all that happens or does not happen during what can be a prolonged stay.

My angelic visitors may have been there to offer me courage and additional support, or to reaffirm that there was no quitting—not with my new heart almost at hand.

When my new heart did come, bringing with it a new lease on life, it seemed to unlock my mind to new opportunities and philosophies. For her part, Joan became more and more spiritual; she urged me to try things I never would have considered before, such as attempting to communicate with the "beyond." We learned a lot, and we opened up our hearts and minds wide. Don't be afraid to expose yourself to new ideas and treatments. I don't mean for you to rush out and try these things impulsively, but stay open to learning about them. And you don't have to wait for trouble to hit before you start learning about what's out there for you. This doesn't mean giving yourself over to every "quack" you run across. It does mean that an open mind now might avoid "open heart" later!

A medical intuitive is a counselor who specializes in perceiving and treating the physical, emotional, relational and career issues of clients. Susan Klopfstein of Irvine, California, is a gifted medical and spiritual intuitive. A medical intuitive is not recommended as a replacement for a medical treatment, but to complement it. I have related elsewhere in the book about the discovery that I was literally bleeding to death and the doctors were having a very difficult time locating the specific cause of the problem and its location. They spent three days conducting every test known, trying to locate the source of the bleeding. The night before the final, scheduled re-test of my intestine, our medical intuitive told Joan that the source of the blood was hidden behind a fold next to the valve. Sure enough, that's where it was. A good guess? Maybe. But it is a fact that she was able to locate something a whole strew of doctors could not. Perhaps it was a good guess, but we continue to use her services and we continue to be amazed at her performance and accuracy.

*

For the most part, we've been discussing what to do so that you may prevent hospitalization or acute care, or so that you'll be prepared as well as possible, should trouble arise. In the second part of the book, we'll turn to what you need to know and what you should do if you find yourself in the hospital. And by now, I hope you'll agree that, with all my experience in hospitals of all shapes and sizes, I'm the right man to give you some guidance in this area! I just hope you'll never need it! But if you do, you and those you love will be ready.

# Part Two:
# When the Need For Care Arises

# Chapter Five:
# Dick's Fourth Rule:
# Demand Attention

Okay, you did everything we talked about … and you still landed in the hospital.

Even after taking the steps to know yourself better than your doctor does, build a team and cultivate communication, and think outside the box, you find yourself hospitalized due to circumstances beyond your control.

My message to you is simple: *don't despair!*

Life is unpredictable, and the only way to get through an unexpected crisis is to meet it with a positive outlook. Although the first three steps in my system deal with action you can begin to take before a hospitalization occurs (and continue to do during that hospitalization), the next three chapters will present actions that you can take specifically while you are in the hospital. These are concepts that helped carry me through major healthcare upheavals, including a four-month stretch on a hospital bed while I waited for a new heart. I found these ideas to be tried and true. I hope they will be equally powerful for you.

The first and most essential step to take when you enter the hospital is to remain engaged with your own care. As long as you are alert and able, you must not become passive. Put simply, there are too many patients and too few doctors at any hospital for you to relinquish responsibility for your own well-being. This means that you must, at every stage of your hospitalization, *demand attention*.

Let me show you what I mean. After my experience with the 1984 Olympics, I was approached by Harry Usher, who was Peter Ueberroth's number two man. Harry had been one of my personal lawyers. It was 1985, and he had become the commissioner of the United States Football League and was busy building the League. The owners threw out the owner of the Los Angeles Express, and they needed a fill-in "owner" for the team. Harry asked if I would do it, and I said, sure. Every guy dreams of owning a big league team someday, and here I became an owner without having to pay millions!

My office was in West L.A. at a school with practice fields available. One day, I felt lousy and kept getting worse. I was having chest pains and severe headaches to the point that we wound up calling an ambulance to transport me to a nearby hospital. While I was being processed there, they kept trying to reach my doctor, who was in Newport Beach. He was out to lunch, so they placed me in a room to await his return. I waited for more than an hour—no doctor. Then a miracle occurred. A cardiologist from another hospital dropped by to see a patient, and was asked to look in on me, as well. He worked at the hospital where I had been admitted, as well as a second hospital in close proximity, and he truly had been jogging by to check on things there, get some exercise, and go on about his day.

After checking me over briefly, his immediate assessment was that I was having a major heart attack. He asked if I would approve if they moved me to his other hospital so they could treat me properly. I agreed, of course, so off we went in another ambulance. There they quickly found out that a blockage had formed and was choking off much-needed blood to a section of my heart. They injected me with something that dissolved the blockage. I had been literally just minutes from death's door, and if that doctor hadn't stumbled upon me, I would have been a goner for sure. As it was, I lost about twenty-five percent of my heart muscle. But I lived. The lesson in this instance: if you aren't getting the proper attention—whether in a waiting room or elsewhere—do whatever it takes to demand attention.

## Choose the Right Hospital for You

As my story shows, you do have a say in which hospitals receive your valuable business—so exercise your choice! As you pick a hospital, keep in mind that hospitals generally fall into several categories. There are teaching hospitals where they teach interns and visiting doctors. These are generally good if you can get under the wing of one of the principal doctors and ensure that he or she pays attention to you. Then there are general hospitals that serve everyone, and these can be great, good or bad, depending on circumstances. Most hospitals have a specialty such as cancer, cardiology, or orthopedics. Some are well known for that specialty. A little research will point you to the one that works best for you. If you already have a specialist, he or she will be on the staff of one or more hospitals and will be able to direct you to one that suits your needs.

In the event of an emergency, there won't be time to hem and haw over which hospital you'd prefer. You will be taken to the closest care center available. It is far better to go by ambulance than to drive yourself or have someone drive you. The immediacy of care you'll receive, compared to walk-in emergency room service, might be a major factor in your survival. If you have time, call your family doctor. It is far better if he calls the hospital in advance and arranges for check-in. Waiting time for ER service ranges up to 5-20 hours in many hospitals—time that can make or break your health. Anything you can do to increase your speed of admittance is critical.

## Secure Adequate Nursing Assistance

Once you're admitted, one of the first things you or your caregiver needs to check is the staffing levels. A typical ratio would be one nurse to three patients in the Intensive Care Unit and one nurse for every eight patients in the general hospital. Furthermore, there are usually different ratios between daytime and nighttime coverage, so find out what the ratios are at night. Why is this important? It doesn't take much to back up the nurses' ability to respond to your needs. This is why we recommend that you have a hired nurse or caregiver, or a family member, there during those late hours. The cost isn't much extra money in the scheme of things, but it can be very important to your well-being. A dropped or inaccessible call button can be the difference between getting critical care when you need it and disaster. My wife's insistence on either being there or having a personal nurse there saved my bacon several times. Don't take the chance yourself!

## Find a Professional Caregiver

Because there are so many hours in a day, there are almost an infinite number of things that can go wrong during your hospital stay and while you are recovering. After you are released from critical care and transition to general hospital care, to a nursing home, rehab center, or even your home, you will need constant attention until you have fully recovered. Your spouse can only do so much; one solution is to hire a professional caregiver.

Through the process of trial and error, Joan and I found an excellent caregiver, Hector Azarcon. He was strong enough to lift me out of my chair or bed, and stubborn enough to overcome my unwillingness to walk, exercise, or do any of the many things that were required to get well. He mastered my maze of medicines and made damn sure that I took them on time … or else! He stayed overnight as needed, gave Joan much-needed breaks for her personal health, and ran the household when she was gone. He also took me to the hospital and stayed with me during the evenings when Joan needed to get away.

The usual appointments with the nurses do not even scratch the surface of what is essential to your recovery. The cost of a personal, professional caregiver is minimal compared to the cost of hospital care, and it is most effective as a quick way to get going again. We have referred Hector to several of our friends who needed help, and everyone had similar successes.

## Go Straight to the Top

After you've established a relationship with your nurses, with whom you'll have the most day-to-day contact, make yourself known to the best physician specializing in your condition. I urge you not to be intimidated or daunted by the task of going to the top, or the lead in command, whenever necessary to make sure you are receiving the proper care and attention. I believe that it's true that anyone you may wish to communicate with is virtually no more than three phone calls away, as long as you know whom you want to reach and are determined to do it. Allow me to illustrate this communication theory with a brief business example from my past.

When I was a young man of twenty-nine, I had bought several companies in the vending machine industry. One of these companies was in Chicago, and it had proven to be very troublesome. The local unions were organized such that two or three different union members from different groups had to go into each one of my machines daily, a process that increased the amount of theft immeasurably. With all the brashness that youth can muster, I reasoned that, since the boss of the unions was Jimmy Hoffa, I would simply go to him. So I wrote him a telegram.

Now, in those days, there was no email. Letters and phone calls were useless when trying to contact somebody important, but telegrams were quite effective. I wrote to Jimmy Hoffa—yes, *the* Jimmy Hoffa—and explained the problem; furthermore, I suggested that I meet with somebody in his organization to resolve the matter. Some weeks later, much to my amazement, I got a phone call, and I was invited to Washington D.C. to meet with Mr. Hoffa personally! It wasn't until I got into his office and realized where I was that I started to get nervous. Nevertheless, I met with Mr. Hoffa and his aides, and we resolved the issue. The message here is that you never know when the big guy is going to respond to a request from anyone. Be persistent and creative, and don't stop until you reach the "top dog."

When you're very sick, the most important relationship of all is the one you have with your doctor and surgeon, the equivalent of the "top dog" or "big boss" at a corporation (and who, like a top executive, is extremely preoccupied, usually overextended and hard to reach). I made a career out of successfully getting through to these types of leaders in industry, and I was able to use similar techniques to connect to my equally busy medical care providers. I can now count on a dozen top medical pros, reachable day or night, because I worked for and earned their friendship.

Sometimes it takes more doing. I never stood outside someone's business office door, day in and day out in, order to make a deal, but I know patients who didn't hesitate to corner their doctors. A friend of mine, Peter Rothschild, became a legend at USC Medical Center for the way he used to track down his surgeons and specialists. He had a transplant four years before I received mine, and he was stuck in the hospital for five months prior to his surgery. Each day at 6 a.m., he would wheel himself down to the hospital lobby and wait by the door for the doctors to arrive. That was the only way he could be sure he'd get his questions answered.

Once you've figured out the right way to connect (which might involve some cleverness like Peter's, or might be as simple as knowing whether your doctors prefer emails or phone calls), always be prepared when that meeting takes place, so that you don't waste anyone's time, including your own. I can't even count the number of times I've suddenly remembered the most crucial question I had for a doctor—ten minutes after he's left my hospital room. Write your questions down as they come to you, and have them on hand when you meet with your doctor.

## Remain Vigilant

Unfortunately, demanding attention sometimes goes beyond simply ensuring that you get a moment of your doctor's time. You may well find yourself in a hospital that is under-staffed and under-funded, and part of your task will be not only to demand attention, but to demand *proper* attention. Human error in the medical field can put your life at risk, so you must work to counteract that risk by being aware and informed. I do not mention this possibility to scare you or to undermine the hard-working people who have committed their lives to keeping us well. It's simply an unfortunate fact of our society that top-quality healthcare is not always possible, given the limited resources of our hospitals and the restrictions imposed by some insurance systems. However, you can guarantee your own vigilance, and you have every right to voice your concerns when something seems amiss.

Here's a story from Joan that illustrates this point:

> During one of Dick's visits to the ER, he was in great pain and needed morphine. A nurse came in to put an I.V. in his arm, and as she was putting her gloves on, she dropped one on the floor of the ER To my amazement, she quickly picked it up, and put it back on! I said, "Aren't you going to change your gloves?" and when she asked, "Why?" I said, "Because you dropped a glove on the floor." She promptly replied, "No, I didn't!"

I still get goose pimples when I think of it. But I really believe that she did not know that she had done it; it was an involuntary reaction, like a reflex, because it happened so quickly. But who knows how many times she might have done that or something similar in the past that went unnoticed, and what type of problems may have resulted for patients? Could there be a dirtier floor in Newport Beach than the one in a hospital's Emergency Room? And there was Dick, a transplant recipient, which means he was an immune-suppressed patient. Anybody could get a staph infection or worse from a careless mistake like that, but with Dick and his immune system, I just was not about to let it slide. You simply can't; you have to speak up and demand proper treatment. It can save your life.

As ever, this same concept applies in the business world. Here's what I mean: I could be $90,000,000 richer today. That's right, ninety million dollars wealthier. A day doesn't pass that I don't reflect on that. I'm sure that doesn't surprise you! We all have learned hard-knock lessons in life, and some of those more have been costly than others; some health-wise, some emotionally, and others financially. This major financial upset all came down to two basic factors: failing to read the fine print on a contract and relying on poor legal advice. Had I been 100 percent healthy at the time (I suffered my second heart attack in the same year), I might have caught the oversight myself. Let me give you the nutshell version of what happened.

I owned a 495,000-acre ranch in central California, which is now the site of a Crystal Geyser bottling plant. Essentially, I didn't protect my underlying water supply from being accessed by a former business partner who bought the adjacent land, took my water, and then made a sweet deal with Crystal Geyser. That's one super "oops," wouldn't you agree?

Again, there are lessons to be learned and cross-applied, if you're willing to use the wisdom you've gained from past experience. In the hospital environment, you'll find that no detail is too small to demand your utmost attention: a dropped glove, medication dosages, innocuous procedures, and on and on. In fact, studies show there is a relatively high incidence of patients today contracting some type of infection after or during a hospital stay. Consider a 2006 study by the respected Institute of Medicine in Washington, D.C., which reported that there are 400,000 preventable drug-related injuries in hospitals, costing at least $3.5 billion. You and your personal support team must stay alert, especially in general care, where nurse-to-patient ratios are higher than in the ICU and mistakes can happen more easily.

Technicians might have the best intentions when performing procedures, but if they're in a hurry and haven't consulted your physicians or the head nurses on the floor, errors can happen. Prior to my heart transplant, I was in intensive care getting a line inserted in my arm to monitor my heart, and the technician ignored the head nurse's orders by performing the procedure in my room instead of a sterile setting. She also made the incision in the wrong arm, resulting in a life-threatening infection. My chest filled with fluid, my lungs collapsed and I nearly died. Fortunately, they were able to drain my chest in time to relieve the pressure, but that was way too close.

Sometimes the pain and suffering many patients endure could be avoided if only doctors would listen. Before my second bypass, my wife and I were concerned that my blood was too thin to endure the surgery and I might bleed too much. The doctors argued that they wanted to keep to their schedule, so we decided to let them operate, against our better judgment. I was on that table an interminable eleven hours, and Joan had to make calls to round up friends to donate blood. I went home to recover, but after a few days, I began coughing uncontrollably. I had a blood clot, and was ordered back to the hospital. Joan and I learned this lesson the hard way: Listen to your doctors, but never forget, the final say belongs to you.

## The Sobering Statistics

While Americans arguably have the top medical system in the world—highly skilled physicians, unparalleled technology and aftercare—it is a system seriously flawed by human error and lax oversight. Sadly, patients who place 100 percent of their trust in their physicians and hospitals might be putting their lives at risk if they don't pay attention to details and manage their own care.

The documentation is substantial to support this contention. In January 2007, the leading independent healthcare ratings company, *HealthGrades* (see www.healthgrades.com) issued its fifth annual hospital quality and clinical excellence study. The survey rates U.S. hospitals for clinical excellence; the findings were alarming. A survey of the Medicare beneficiaries admitted to U.S. hospitals between 2003 and 2005 showed that 158,264 lives may have been saved and 12,310 patients may have avoided major complications if they had been treated at hospitals identified as Distinguished Hospitals for Clinical Excellence. When researchers zeroed in on coronary bypass surgery, a patient's chances of dying increased by seventy-three percent if treated in a one star-rated hospital, compared to a five star-rated hospital. In other words, go to the wrong hospital and your mortality risk can increase.

Government agencies charged with monitoring the numerous transplant programs have failed miserably. My heart transplant cost more than one million dollars; you'd think, at that price, anyone needing a transplant would be given a fair shake and would receive the finest care. But in October of 2006, the *L.A. Times* exposed an organ donor network that is in terrible shape. The controversy has cost lives and entangled some of California's leading hospitals, serving as a dire alert for patients and their families.

The blame lies with individual hospitals and the organization charged by the federal government with overseeing transplant procedures and organ distribution, the United Network for Organ Sharing. The *Times* exposé revealed that UNOS is hampered by weak oversight and secret investigations that seem more determined to protect hospitals than the transplant patients expecting top-notch care. The University of California Medical Center scandal is a case in point. My good friend and colleague, John Rader, was a patient in the liver transplant program there. One spring day in 2005, he opened the morning newspaper and read that the program he was enrolled in had been without a full-time liver transplant surgeon for a year. The program was in chaos; not only were patients mired on the waitlist, but others were dying. In all, thirty-five patients passed away as the hospital rejected scores of viable organs. The program was shut down, and John was transferred to USC's program; but there, he had to go to the end of the line. They weren't able to get him a liver in time. He died in 2006.

If the UCI scandal were an isolated case, I probably wouldn't have written this book. I'm distressed at the dangers lurking in our American medical facilities: sacred codes of conduct for dispensing precious organs are being violated; medication is dispensed incorrectly; and hospitals are admitting organ transplant patients they cannot service, costing lives and billions of dollars.

In Wisconsin, the Children's Hospital in Milwaukee ignored UNOS's repeated demands to shut down its lung program in 2004. Although the hospital wasn't performing any lung transplants, it kept children on its waitlist anyway, preventing them from getting surgery elsewhere. The hospital was performing too few surgeries and had a high death rate. UNOS came down on the hospital, but only put it on confidential probation, the *Times* reported. Even though the hospital performed just one transplant in four years, there were still six children on the waitlist.

In the transplant world, there was supposed to be a code: those most in need got the organs first. Violate the code, and a hospital risked losing its status as a transplant center. But that code is being blatantly broken. At L.A.'s St. Vincent Medical Center's liver transplant program (this is where I underwent my first heart bypass), federal officials learned that the staff improperly arranged a liver transplant for a Saudi national with an organ designated for someone higher on the waitlist. Then they tried to cover it up. The liver transplant program was closed down in 2006, and in October, the fallout extended to its heart transplant program when hospital officials closed its doors as well.

Organ donors have something to fear, too. In February 2006, a dying twenty-six-year-old California man may have had his death accelerated by a San Luis Obispo transplant surgeon, brought in to harvest his organs. The doctor is under investigation by state and federal authorities for possibly speeding up the patient's death by ordering his body to be pumped full of narcotic painkillers, all in the presence of six other professionals.

Temple University Medical Center figured out another way to hasten surgery for heart transplant patients: it just reported them sicker than they actually were, bumping them higher on the list at the expense of patients at other hospitals. This went on for several years, yet when it was discovered, the only penalty was a slap on the wrist: confidential probation, which was lifted in 2006.

The code has been circumvented in other ways. An *L.A. Times* investigation in 2006 showed that the speed of your organ transplant and your odds of getting a new organ before you die may depend on where you live rather than on how sick you are, especially if you need a liver. For example, a liver transplant candidate who must wait four years for an organ in New York may only have to wait two weeks for a liver if he relocates to Florida. Why? Some states with abundant organ supplies enacted laws preventing organ export without first offering the body parts to in-state patients, regardless of where the need was greatest.

I witnessed firsthand the stagnation and mismanagement inherent in many hospitals when, six years after my heart transplant, I was back in the hospital again, this time undergoing surgery to remove blood clots from my groin. As I mentioned earlier, complications due to a nurse's error arose, and I was later re-hospitalized with a hematoma and a staph infection. I hated going back, but it gave me the opportunity to put my rules to the test. There was plenty to be concerned about: the training of hospital staff, sad to say, hadn't gotten much better, and parts of the basic infrastructure hadn't changed in six years. I'm referring to such fundamental things as telephone service and nurse call mechanisms, which are crucial during the course of an extended hospital stay. There does seem to be a light at the end of the tunnel, however: the changes are finally coming as USC buys its hospital back from a for-profit company. This shift was underway as of 2008.

As USC exemplifies, the news isn't all bad. USC and other hospitals are stepping up and making changes to improve their patient care and reduce potentially dangerous medical errors. Many recently improved a major area of hospital care by utilizing computers to assist in administering medication—no small matter when you consider that nationwide, hundreds of thousands of patients are harmed each year from medication errors. Saddleback Memorial in Laguna Hills, California went completely paperless to cut down on such common mistakes as misinterpreting illegible handwritten instructions and misunderstanding lab test requests because of verbal miscues. The UC Irvine hospital transplant program cleaned house and aggressively recruited new surgeons to resurrect its much-maligned kidney and liver transplant programs. This was not in time to save my friend John Rader's life, but it is a start.

There is a public perception that the U.S. medical industry is "top drawer." What can possibly go wrong? Nothing, right?

*Wrong.* Everything can go wrong. The prevailing thought is that if somebody dies, it's just "because"—but I'm here to tell you, it's not. There are many deaths that could have been prevented. It's absolutely essential that you manage your own care and have a team in place to help you. Don't count on our medical system to be foolproof. Ask questions, challenge the line of command, and support public policy aimed at improving medical care and working conditions for hospital staff. Your life may very well depend on it.

\*

Despite all the complications, the potential dangers, and fallible medical care, I am forever grateful that I received the transplant and have recovered so well from that procedure. I would be remiss if I didn't take a moment to talk about smoking, especially as it relates to my transplant. If I had smoked, I probably wouldn't have been accepted, at my age, for a transplant. Several times during my medical challenges, many doctors told me that I would not have been as successful, had I smoked. It blows my mind to see people of all ages and with all kinds of medical problems smoking. Smoking is a voluntary death sentence. If you smoke, do whatever it takes to shake the habit.

# Chapter Six:
# Dick's Fifth Rule:
# Develop a Daily Routine

As I've shared with you already, I spent four long months at USC Medical Center awaiting my heart transplant. That amount of time in a hospital is not only depressing, it's dangerous to your health, especially with the imminent, looming potential of infection. Compound all that with the natural buildup of accompanying stress, plus an ever-weakening heart, and you have a pretty certain recipe for disaster on your hands. But I survived, and I want to share with you how and why I believe I did.

Contending with the day-to-day minutiae of living in the hospital can become monumental. Something very menial and commonplace, like going to the restroom, turned into a half-hour ordeal because of all the tubes running in and out of my body;

it took forever to partially disengage myself from that tangled mess and get across the room. In four months, I only managed to get outdoors four times, although Joan and I became masters at changing rooms—packing and unpacking seventeen times—as the hospital moved me from one bed to the next to keep me eligible for a new heart. I could have sworn someone had tattooed the *Mayflower Transit* moving emblem on my wheelchair!

There were some humorous moments, and thank God for those, because comic relief is extremely welcome in such long, drawn-out ordeals. One example that stands out in my mind from that time period is of the stern young nurse who would march into my room and demand, in no uncertain terms, "Pee for me now!" It's funny in retrospect, but at the time, she drove me nuts. She wouldn't leave without a full cup! I finally was able to convince the head nurse that she had to be replaced, and mercifully, they complied with my request.

You would think with all that downtime, I could have written a book and read ten more, or at the very least, conducted a little business by phone. I fully expected to do all of this, but being connected to so much equipment and doped up on medication, those simple things became impossible tasks. The highlight of my day was usually mealtime, especially if Joan was able to bring in some decent food. You know how it is in hospitals and other such institutions—*anything* tastes better than what they serve in the hospital!

When you're faced with an extended stay in the hospital, in spite of all the people around you, you are going to be left alone a lot of the time. Loneliness is an absolute killer if it's not handled correctly. You might be drugged up enough that you're out of it and you don't care. But I can tell you that, if your mind is still active, each and every 24 hours feels like an eternity.

The hustle and bustle of activities during the day still leaves you facing a long night where you stare at the ceiling and wonder if you're ever going to get out of there. Preparing yourself mentally for these periods of time is an absolute must, and there's no definite way of dealing with the problem. I find that having things to think about that are positive in nature, like your family, will help pass the time. Those of you who can face that loneliness with positivity and the knowledge that it's not forever will get through the hospital ordeal much better than others.

I found that, on the other hand, the constant interruption of my sleep or naps with needless repetitive tests could drive a man to drink—that is, if there were any place to get a drink! During the four months I spent in Intensive Care waiting for a heart, I had about four or five teams of people who looked after me for one reason or another. Each team seemed to order its own series of tests, so I was constantly being checked not only for vital signs, but for every conceivable body activity. I was being awakened—I thought needlessly—over and over again between the hours of midnight and 6 AM. After appealing to my lead physician, they finally reduced this to one or two tests during that time period, which enabled me to have much more sleep and get the rest that I needed.

The funny thing was, when I was admitted to USC to get my new heart, I only planned on staying a few weeks, tops. "No worries, I'll get my new heart and be back to work in no time at all," I glibly assured my associates. Little did I know I was in for four tedious months of utter boredom with not only a weak body, but an active mind that raced around in circles like a dog chasing its tail. Lying in bed for so long, I lost fifty pounds and my legs and arms lost all muscle tone and strength. I'd never trade places with a cancer patient, but at least their schedule is somewhat set with treatments such as chemo and radiation, or what I call "time-certain events." There is no such agenda for transplant patients waiting for an organ.

For me to live, someone else had to die, another mind-numbing realization I tried to bury away deep in the recesses of my mind. Sometimes I heard helicopters roar overhead like on the TV show *M.A.S.H.*, and I'd think, "Are they bringing me my heart? Is it my turn?" My hopes were dashed time after time. Finally, I realized I wouldn't make it unless I developed a code of discipline to get through each day.

Cliché as it sounds, my first and most important rule is to take one day at a time and never to think about tomorrow or yesterday. I fought the urge to look too far ahead and compartmentalized my life into small segments. Only at night, as I was falling asleep, did I think about the following day, much of which was set in stone by routine tests, tasks such as bathing  meals, and preparing for doctor's rounds by jotting down questions in advance with Joan. I prepared for my day the same way a CEO does—I just didn't look too far ahead. That way, I could measure my day in segments and make time to celebrate small victories to keep my spirits up and confidence high.

To me, the most important thing during my hospital "incarceration" was my secret stash of Ben & Jerry's ice cream. I kept it in a small refrigerator we were able to share with the nurses. For bedridden folks, the little things count for a lot. Every now and then, to break my steady adherence to routine, I would reward myself when something went right. A test that came back with a favorable result was cause for a dish of Ben & Jerry's. On really special occasions, the nurses took me outside to experience the sunshine—but only four times in four months.

Two capable nurses (Joan Stevens [left] and Kara
Fox) make sure Dick is well-cared for.

# Chapter Seven:
# Dick's Sixth Rule:
# Never Give Up

Before I went into the hospital to wait for my heart, I went out with Joan for New Year's Eve 2000. I could barely walk across the street, let alone dance. But that was what Joan wanted, one last dance. She didn't say what everyone else was thinking—that I literally appeared to be on my last legs. She grabbed my arm and we headed for the dance floor. I know what was going through people's minds: "Dead Man Walking." Nonetheless, I dragged myself out to the parquet, took Joan in my arms, and we danced to *Auld Lang Syne*. I finished the dance in one piece, but two weeks later, I suffered my fifth and final heart attack—while getting a haircut at the Balboa Bay Club, of all places. Finally, I was deemed sick enough to get a crack at a heart transplant.

I carried that same attitude with me from the dance floor into the hospital bed. Apart from sticking to the code of discipline that I described in the previous chapter, the thing that kept me alive was actively insisting to myself that I stay positive. Be prepared: keeping high spirits in a hospital is tough. You must take your inspiration wherever and whenever you can find it. I found mine in the next room over from a young woman suffering with cystic fibrosis. She was just twenty-three years old and had traveled down from Canada with her parents. She was preparing to undergo a double lung-heart transplant, a procedure her parents told me was not performed in Canada. It just broke my heart—what was left of it, anyway—to see that poor girl endure such suffering at such a young age. She had her transplant about a month after I arrived, and she didn't go home until after I had my transplant in May. Here I was, sixty-nine years old (and that was *old* for a transplant patient). I had already lived a rich, full life that was about to be extended again, thanks to our country's medical technology. I felt extremely lucky, so I was motivated to take the setbacks in stride and wait my turn.

As I lay in bed, I also had ample time to think about the fates that befell my father and my older brother, who also died of a heart condition and had refused to go to the hospital when he needed treatment most. I'd like to share my brother's story here. Tom had an arrhythmia, which is an uneven beating of the heart muscle. It did not cause him problems in his younger years, but popped up as a concern when he was in his sixties. Arrhythmia happens when the heart muscle starts beating erratically; usually it's treated by drugs. When Tom was being treated for the arrhythmia, he should have gone into the hospital for extensive tests. He chose to postpone that option, and as a consequence, he passed away in his sleep at home. If he had put himself into the hospital for observation, he probably would be alive today. During the four months I spent in the hospital, remembering my brother and knowing that I was doing everything in my power to take charge of my condition kept me ready to face each new day.

I didn't draw inspiration only from my medical experiences. Overcoming crazy odds in the business world is an integral part of my M.O., and this gave me the wherewithal to survive five heart attacks, two bypass surgeries and, finally, a transplant. The ability to pull together a deal when the situation appears hopeless has taught me never to give up hope, and never to look at anything as totally impossible. I remember one business transaction that was three years in the making—a condo project on Catalina Island, off the coast of Los Angeles, on property that was owned by the Wrigley family. (You know, the chewing gum empire?) It took me three years to get a meeting with Mr. Wrigley, but I was confident and accustomed to waiting my turn. When I did get my appointment, in twenty minutes he agreed to my proposal of a fifty-year lease to build condos and a leisure club, now known as Hamilton Cove. Talk about doubling your pleasure while creating something that would double others' pleasure and fun as well!

I also learned from deals that did not go my way. At age twenty-seven, I tried to put together a group to buy a successful wiring and cable product company. I knew the seller; he was many years my senior and thought I was a nice young man. He gave me thirty-six hours to put a team in place to finance the purchase. At first, I struck out with a New York bank, but the next day I landed a meeting with a San Francisco group that agreed to back me. Alas, I was a day late; the seller had accepted a competing bid the day before. Although I was outgunned from the start, the fact that I almost pulled it off and didn't give up gave me confidence in the years ahead when other opportunities beckoned. Bottom line lesson? Keep after it!

I tell you this story because I want to make it clear that there's no quitting in the transplant business, either. You need to be prepared for false alarms and disappointment. One night, a nurse roused me and said they were going to prep me for surgery—my new heart was arriving by helicopter! Joan jumped out of her chair, called our friends, and asked them to please say prayers and think positive thoughts.

Six hours passed as they tested and inspected the heart. When I saw my surgeon, his face looked drawn and he wasn't smiling. I could tell by his body language that the news was bad. My new heart turned out to be a reject: it had tumors. Joan had to call everyone back to tell them the operation was off. I sank into a depression. We waited another three weeks before another heart became available, and this time we kept it to ourselves. I received the heart of a thirty-year-old man, which was strong and healthy. It still serves me extremely well today.

While waiting those four months in the hospital, I had the opportunity to become quite close to the doctors on my team and privy to some conversations between them. When the time for my transplant finally arrived, I knew that the heart had come from a nearby hospital because the doctors were talking about who was going to go over and do the harvesting. Later, I learned the name of the hospital, and in subsequent conversations, I found out that the donor was a thirty-year-old male. Obviously, it wouldn't have been too much of a task for me to track down who passed away at that hospital on that date. But I chose not to do so, and I still believe my choice was a wise one. At one point, doctors

86

encouraged the recipients to write a letter to the transplant service to be forwarded to the donor's family. I did write such a letter, but never heard back from anyone, which is not atypical.

Presently, most of the medical community feels that it's not a good idea to contact the donor's family directly, because, of course, it may be an extremely emotional situation. You naturally want to reach out and thank those individuals who are responsible for your being alive. I've read about many instances where the donor's families have met with recipients, and most of these meetings turned out well. But the potential dangers of such a contact might override the emotional advantages. Most of the medical community is now concerned about the emotional effects on the donor's family of meeting with the recipient. The general consensus seems to hold that it's not a prudent idea.

Ultimately, I came out of this intense medical ordeal with a new, healthy heart, wide open to the future. I am eternally grateful for the second chance. If you find yourself in my shoes, take a deep breath, and keep things in perspective. Your hospitalization is not a setback or a stroke of bad luck. It's an opportunity to reclaim your life, to grasp your survival in your own hands. The big, life-or-death picture is overwhelming, so take each hurdle as it comes. All you have to do is get through today. You'll find, amazing as it is, that if you are disciplined with yourself and you insist on taking things one step at a time, the silver lining of any situation will simply surface for you without effort and without fooling yourself. This is crucial. This is the mindset that will pull you through.

Now you have them: my six rules for surviving and thriving, no matter what your medical history or diagnosis. Of course, none of this is meaningful until you put it into practice. So don't delay.

As the insurance salesman tells you, better a year too soon than a day late. And if you do put these ideas into practice, you'll find yourself healthier ... and safer ... than ever.

In the concluding chapter, I'd like to share my wish for you.

# Chapter Eight:
# My Wish for You

You might just live to be 110 years old and in great health.

That's my wish for you.

But don't bet on it.

The likelihood few of us want to face is that we aren't going to live forever, and we may well find ourselves on a bumpy road in what little time we have left. The good news is that this doesn't mean defeat or helplessness. In fact, it means you have an opportunity to take control of your life, your attitude, and your health, and you'll find a wealth of joy and wisdom in the process.

I hope that you have found our book to be an interesting and thought-provoking start toward a healthier life. There is so much to think about and to do to give yourself every opportunity to enjoy a long and fruitful life. The most important thing is to have the will to live, no matter what cards the gods deal you. With a will to live, you can overcome many big hurdles. The next crucial element is to *be prepared*. In this book we have given you the essentials to helping you survive catastrophic events: learning to gather the information you need about your own healthcare, building the support network that will sustain you, accepting new modes of caring for and healing your body, demanding the quality care you deserve, and never giving up. Now don't just nod your head. Get off your rear-end and do those things that are so essential to your survival.

Your doctors are neither magicians nor mind-readers. You hinder them in their jobs if you remain passive. They need your active vigilance, cooperation, and insight to keep you well. So, know yourself better than your doctor does. Keep tabs on your own health and be prepared to ask questions and participate with your doctor when you go in for an appointment. Your doctor will be relieved to have an involved and curious patient for a change, and your health will benefit—guaranteed.

The absolute imperative of having a team to support you in times of need is stressed throughout this book, as you'll find that it is in life—if you're paying attention. To those of you who do not have a ready-made team of family close to you, there are many ways to build your own team. Most of us have friends or associates who may be without family, or others who can be counted on in need. Many of these people may be in the same boat. There may be an opportunity for several of you to enter into an agreement that you will all become teammates if one of you has a problem—sharing the future load, so to speak. Once you have your group gathered, you will need to brief every member on all the emergency information you each have. Be sure to include their contact numbers on your emergency list that you now carry on you, so your doctors will know to contact them. Think carefully about whom you entrust to make medical decisions for you.

Don't close your mind to any alternative avenues that may be of assistance to you. The accepted cures of today were the odd-ball remedies of yesterday. You are only making room for growth for yourself if you are prepared to explore every possible avenue on your own path to wellness. If you do your research and ensure that all treatments you undertake are in line with your doctor's recommendations and are not counteracting one another, you increase your odds of success exponentially by your willingness to explore.

No system is worthy of your unquestioning trust. More than likely, your doctors are good doctors and your hospital staff usually tries its best. But a system is a system, and it is naïve to place your blind faith in it. Demand the attention you need. Get behind the wheel and make sure that your care providers know you are willing to work hard alongside them. If you're prepared to put in the effort, your medical team will be more able to repay your efforts with their skill and attention.

Keep in mind that as you move toward wellness you will be confronted by a number of new challenges, none seemingly connected to your original medical problem. As an example, recipients of new organs will be given a lifelong prescription of anti-rejection drugs which lower your immune system. These drugs, in turn, can result in skin problems such as acne, or even skin cancer which may or may not create a new set of problems for you. It is a small price to pay for the gift of a new life. Deal with these problems as they come but just remember...you must never give up!

Last, but not least, by any stretch of the imagination: take one day at a time and stay positive. A positive outlook does not mean putting on blinders to your situation, and it's not something that you are simply born with or without. It requires mental discipline. Be honest with yourself and keep reminding yourself to change your usual habits and thought patterns. The more you cultivate positivity, the more it will arise on its own—and your body will follow suit with your mind. Embracing persistence and never giving up is the only path to wellness.

We hope that you have been able to glean from our story some ideas that will help you. We all have many more tomorrows to enjoy—with a little luck, some thinking and preparation, and the ultimate desire to live.

Enjoy your life, and may it be a long one!

Joan & Dick

# Our Medical Team

I have listed the key members of our team, and several of them have been gracious enough to express their thoughts on health and the continuing struggle to provide better care, and some things you can do to help yourself.

**John Storch, M.D.**, Internal Medicine, Board Certified 1988, University of Southern California Medical School. Dr. Storch has been the captain of our team and coordinator of our physical health for 20 years.

**Uri Elkayam, M.D.**, director of the Heart Failure Program, Professor of Medicine and Professor of Obstetrics and Gynecology at the University of Southern California in Los Angeles. He specializes in heart failure and it treatment.

**Mark L. Barr, M.D.**, is associate professor of Cardiothoracic Surgery (with tenure) at the University of Southern California, Keck School of Medicine, where he is co-director of Cardiothoracic Transplantation and Associate Director of Cardiothoracic Surgical Research. He obtained his medical degree from Mount Sinai School of Medicine in New York and completed 10 years of postgraduate residency at New York University and Columbia University. Dr. Barr has authored more than 150 peer-reviewed publications and book chapters in the fields of cardiothoracic surgery and heart and lung transplantation. Dr. Barr personally has taken care of my new heart for eight years.

**Felicia Barr** heads up the nursing staff that cares for everyone undergoing a transplant operation at USC. She is a wonderful coordinator.

**Vaughn A. Starnes, M.D.**, is Hastings Distinguished Professor and Chairman of the Department of Cardiothoracic Surgery and the Director of the Cardiothoracic Residency Training Program at the Keck School of Medicine. Dr. Starnes was responsible for actually performing my heart transplant.

**Fred A. Weaver, M.D.**, holds the title of Professor of Surgery at the Keck School of Medicine of the University of Southern California. Dr. Weaver's education includes a Bachelor of Science and Doctor of Medicine degrees from the University of Southern California. He is currently the Chief of Vascular Surgery and Medical Director of the Vascular Laboratory at USC University Hospital. He is known for his challenging teaching style, scholarly contributions, and devotion to the practice of Vascular Surgery. Dr. Weaver performed my groin surgery and guided my aftercare.

**Virginia Cooke, M.D.**, is a fine vascular surgeon who, after sustaining an injury, became an outstanding expert in bio-identical hormone therapy. She is a nutrition expert and does research on how drugs affect the body and how hormones are needed.

**Mitra K. Nadim, M.D.** is the Assistant Professor of Medicine, and Associate Director of the Hypertension Service. She is also the Renal System Chair for 2nd year medical students at USC Keck School of Medicine, Department of Medicine, Division of Nephrology.

# Appendix One:
# An Interview with Dr. Cooke

If you've learned anything from my advice, it's that you've got to take charge, do your homework, and make your own inquiries. So don't just take my word for any of this! In the following appendices, you'll find interviews with the highly qualified members of my medical team who have kept me alive all these years. I hope you'll find that their insights add to your arsenal of tools for taking charge of your health.

**Dr. Cooke:**    I was educated at Columbia in New York; as an undergraduate I studied biochemistry. Prior to that, I was a college drop-out. I lived in the Midwest and started out studying a variety of subjects back there, but dropped out, got married and experienced some complications during my first pregnancy. As a consequence, I met some great physicians and thought, "Wow!

That's what I want to do." So, I decided to quit my job and I went back to school.

I went to Columbia in New York for general studies, and really wanted to go there for medical school. It was an excellent school, but was rather hard for me to get in. I was thirty-two years old, the oldest woman they had ever accepted, and also the only woman with a child. It took two interviews for me to get in. One of the things about Columbia that I value is that it teaches you to think independently; I think that's a very unique aspect of their educational process. I've met people from schools like Harvard or Yale, and they just don't think the same way. At that point in time, they taught their students to take the position that it doesn't matter where you come in on the project, you need to review all of the information and think about it as though no one has ever thought anything about this case before. That way, you can bring a fundamentally new approach to the problem. In this way, you may see something nobody else has thought of or noticed. They educated their students to openly question professors instead of kowtowing to the Grand Poobahs. In other words, they were very open to questioning and encouraged people to do that.

As a result, it made sort of a rebellious thinker out of me, medically speaking. I was studying cell biology at a time in Columbia when they had just finished doing the electron microscopy work, whereby they could actually see cell membranes and identify more molecular structures. This gave a better understanding of cells, organelles and things that are way too small to be appreciated under regular, old-fashioned microscopic magnification. So they really started studying a lot of cellular processes, and that's what I thought I was going to do in medical school, take that information and use it for medical problem-solving. But here's what actually happened. During the first year of medical school, you have a giant vocabulary lesson and learn the language of that field of study. The second year you learn the language of pathology and how things go wrong. And the third and fourth years you try to relate it to sick people and problem-solving. But there's no place in those four years for biochemistry and cell biology. And there was an extensive emphasis on the use of pharmaceutical agents.

Today, I think doctors are pretty much relegated to the role of a waiter or waitress with a pad who are expected to say, "May I take your order?" People watch TV or go online and find a drug they want to use, and are encouraged to "Go to your doctor and see if this drug's right for you," which usually translates to, "I want this drug now!" Someone called me the other day and said, "I want a doctor who can prescribe this, that and the other," and I said, "Well, if you want to become a patient of mine, I'd certainly be happy to look at that, if that's what you want to do." He said, in a very disappointed voice, "Oh, you can't prescribe those for me right now?" and I said, "No." See, everybody is drug-happy.

**Dick**:       Viagra may be the leading criminal there.

**Dr. Cooke**:   Well, that's a very scary drug because nobody seems to check the person's testosterone level or anything else. It's a systemic basal active drug, which means it will affect blood level constriction everywhere in your body, not just down in that one little place. I'm amazed more people don't have heart attacks from it. Perhaps they're just not reported.

Anyway, I went to medical school thinking I would be doing more of what I actually do today, but it never happened. I didn't want to become a medical doctor because I sat in a number of clinics and heard doctors talking to patients, trying to get them to do certain things and eat certain ways to treat their hypertension and other conditions. It's like trying to kick a mule into a barn! Nobody wants to do it; they just want the pills and then they want to go home. Or some of them get depressed when you give them a pill. I was not much of a talker back then, but I liked to do things with my hands, so I decided I would be a surgeon. I really was fascinated by vascular surgery, so I did a lot of research in that area as an undergraduate and eventually became a vascular surgeon. It took me a long time—I put in a few extra years there. It was difficult, as a woman. I had my son when I was a pre-med, and then my first daughter between the first and second years of medical school.

First, I became a general surgeon, and then moved west to do a vascular surgery fellowship. I would have been doing a ridiculous amount of surgery, had that continued. Vascular surgery is all emergencies; that's all it is. It can be an exhausting lifestyle. But due to a spinal cord injury, I could no longer operate—my hands and legs were numb for two-and-a-half years. So during my recovery, I started thinking about all those cell biology and biochemical things that I knew about but had never applied. I ran into an older doctor who had been practicing bio-identical hormonal therapy for about thirty-five years, and to his credit, he really educated himself and helped a lot of people. I was a patient of his for awhile, and learned a lot from him; then I went out on my own and started experimenting with using a combination of many of the things that I do now.

**Dick**: So that sets the scene for who you are. I guess the biggest question I have is, what is wrong with our medical system today?

**Dr. Cooke**: Well, unfortunately, there are several ancient myths that predominate thinking where medical problems are concerned. Number One is that a "fountain of youth" does exist, and that myth is very closely tied to another, which ism "There is a magic pill that is going to fix your problem. If you just wait and give us another twenty minutes, we'll develop it and get it on the market, so you'll make it." Also, for every pill, there is a named problem. So that creates separation in reality between you, your body and the consequences of your actions in relation to your body. We are living in a society of people who are grossly disconnected. Most of them don't want to get connected. So the problem, first of all, is that there is an unrealistic expectation and a disconnection from the person and how the problems get generated. At the same time, who makes the largest contribution to the disconnection? The pharmaceutical industry, which makes billions of dollars a year from drugs. In this country, you can only patent something that is not identical to a naturally occurring substance. If you are allowed to get a patent on something, it lasts 40 years, and in rare cases, you can get another 40-year extension. But in general, once you get the patent, you make your money—and in 40 years, everybody else can make the same thing under a different name and sell it.

I'll cite an example. Lipitor was coming up for its fortieth year anniversary this year, and so they were trying to make a drug that would not only lower cholesterol but also lower high blood pressure. On the front page of the *New York Times*—I cannot even believe they printed it—they reported that the study for this new drug had to be canceled, and the drug completely pulled. Why? Because more than 120 people who had participated in the study died. My question was, after ten people died, why was it continued? Because they want to develop that "magic pill"—they want another great big seller.

All of these lipid-lowering drugs are related to a falsehood. They're sold on the premise that cholesterol (you see this on TV commercials) is like hair floating around, getting clogged in the drain. If there's too much hair, like in your drain at home, eventually there's going to be a branch point and the hair will get clogged there and create a blockage. So we have to cut down the hair in circulation, ergo we have to decrease the amount of cholesterol that a person has in their bloodstream. No one bothers to look at the fact that A plus B equals C. Cholesterol is the very molecule that all steroid based hormones are made from, and if you don't have A, you will not make C, and you need C to run your body biochemistry. At the same time, the Number One most sensitive specific indicator of development of atherosclerosis is an amino acid called homocysteine. All this research was done about 40 years ago and was suppressed; it wasn't republished until 1997 in the *New England Journal of Medicine.* It shows that homocysteine is the reason that the natural repair process of cracks in the blood vessel wall turned from a nice, neat patch into some goober blob that happens to contain cholesterol crystals, which look like cornmeal and melted plastic. If you can keep your homocysteine levels low, you will vastly reduce your risk of sudden death from a heart attack due to atherosclerosis. How do you do that? With cheap, water-soluble B vitamins, B6, B12 and folic acid, the enzyme cofactors that convert homocysteine into nontoxic amino acids.

Anyway, that one myth alone generates billions of dollars and keeps millions of people in chemical bondage and illness. This country needs to have a revolution. In my opinion, people need to stop taking drugs and get close to their bodies, figure out what's wrong, and learn how to trick their bodies into working right.

**Dick:**      How do you do that?

**Dr. Cooke:**      There are five doors. There are really ten, but I'll simplify it.

## The Five Doors

1. Endocrine balance

2. Providing the right nutrition for your body

3. Micro-nutrition - Vitamins

4. Stress reduction

5. Exercise

Now we'll look at each one of these doors. You must have endocrine balance—you must have hormones to run your body biochemistry. If you don't have them, it will not work. I've seen this most profoundly now in young women under the age of twenty-five who are taking oral contraceptive pills; because it's a synthetic hormone treatment, it seems to block natural ovarian function almost completely in some people, and puts them artificially into menopause. So they get depressed and cry and they don't know why. Maybe they don't have acne anymore, and their periods aren't heavy, but now they're depressed and they're a mess and can't think straight. Or they gain weight. So they go to a doctor who says, "Oh, you're depressed," and then gives them an antidepressant, which blocks their hormone function even more! You must have hormones, I don't care how old you are, and especially if you're traumatized, or living in a situation where there's environmental pollution. Your body won't run without hormones.

The second door is good food; you must give your body the right nutrition. Depending on your metabolism, you can strategize to stabilize your blood sugar level, but you must support your metabolism. It requires an entire changeover of all the cells in your body every five to 120 days, with the exception of your brain and your spinal cord. So if you think about it in terms of "what's left of me today?" 120 days from now, it's the brain and the spinal cord sitting there, and that's it! People think eating is for pleasure, or because you have to be a certain size or whatever—no! You have a job; your body is like a factory and if you don't put the raw materials in, you're not going to get the quality product out. Your body is constantly trying to meet the demands of making new cells. And if you fail to supply those raw materials, then your body will break down existing structures to get spare parts, just like a salvage yard. Then what you're left with is a dump! You're not feeling good, your body isn't working right, and the parts it's made are kind of faulty anyway, because they weren't made with good stuff, or maybe everything wasn't there. Or maybe you are so bad off that it simply won't make a "new you" at all. How much emphasis is there on eating well?

**Dick:**        Most people don't know how.

**Dr. Cooke:**   Even back in the '80s when I was in medical school, they cut the nutrition section from three weeks to one week because there were too many drugs to study about. See what's happened?

The third door is micro-nutrition; enzyme cofactors, vitamins. Vitamins are enzyme cofactors for biochemical reactions, which assist them to proceed forward to completion. If you don't have them, things won't happen. A basic thing like hair requires collagen; a collagen molecule is three strands, and then it's cross-linked with Vitamin C and Vitamin E and an amino acid named proline. If you're not making any of those things, it's not going to go into cross-linking and make a triple helix, and if there's no triple helix, it's not going to be as strong. We need collagen for everything, not just hair, skin and nails; it's in blood vessel walls, it's everywhere.

So there are a lot of little things your body needs, and you have to attend to giving them to your body. This is all environmentally connected, because we're suffering from vitamin deficiencies in our food sources. This has happened because we chemically fertilize the soil; we put in four things and the plants take out twenty-nine. In the old days, they used to rotate crops and leave things fallow for two years, or perhaps grow soybeans to replenish the soil. Since they no longer do that, the plants you eat are mineral-impoverished, which means you're not going to absorb these vitamin cofactors the way God made you to absorb them. So the next best thing is to take extra. A lot of people say, "Oh, taking vitamins isn't good, you shouldn't do it," but what are you gonna do? You have to do something, like take those B vitamins, or you'll wind up with clogged arteries.

Today, you'd have to eat a couple of bushels of apples a day to keep the doctor away– not just one, which was the case in the early 1900s when that phrase was coined! If you're eating the whole apple, you should know that the skin holds onto concentrated pesticides. So if you don't eat organically produced food, you're going to consume more than a gallon-and-a-half of pesticides annually. Of course, the big linkage to cancer, carcinogens, is assimilation of hydrocarbon substances such as DDT. In this county and others where they used to spray certain crops with DDT, the incidence of breast cancer is way higher than the national average. DDT stays in the water tables for about 120 years, so every day you turn the shower on, you get chemically polluted water, which is absorbed into your skin. Then your liver dutifully tries to detoxify it and change it into hormone-like substances called "xenohormones," which are dummy hormones. These substances, which are also non-biodegradable, compete with your functional hormones for cell-receptor sites. Hormones lock onto cells to tell them what to do. There are many different receptor mechanisms, but to put it simply, it's a lock and key operation. If you stick in the wrong key it won't turn, and it never opens the door. So many cancers are related to that hormone deficiency situation we've created.

Doors four and five are basically amorphous, but the fourth one is definitely related to stress reduction. This is something I learned about while studying surgery. Surgeons are great metabolic experts. A well-respected surgeon wrote a book which, in the first chapter, identified that there's a paradoxical set of reactions that occur when you have a "traumatized" metabolism. Although he doesn't talk about eicosonoids in there, basically there is a paradoxical thing that they observed in trauma patients who, for example, have third degree burns all over the body. You tend to think, "Oh my God, the body's going to work harder and make more stuff and heal," but it doesn't. The paradoxical response is that all normal growth and repair, hormone production, and function is reduced, because the metabolism is dominated by the operative adrenals. It turns out that the essence of body biochemistry is very philosophical. These chemicals, called "eicosonoids" are fatty acids that trigger either a series of reactions that go to cellular warfare, immune response defense, and blood vessel restriction; or they go into a peace-time regrowth and repair. This is kind of the yin and yang of body biochemistry. The way the body is made, each function is mutually exclusive. You cannot be in peace and war simultaneously. So how does that relate to the walking and talking? Obviously, it's been very well-delineated for people who are traumatized and flat on their backs in the ICU. But actually, I took this and applied it to people who are just a little sick, maybe not feeling so good. It turns out that the expression of fear or worry (the old mind/body connection) is the way that we tap into that "warfare and defense" pathway—inadvertently. So when we worry or are fearful, we prevent our bodies from regrowth and repair, and since the demand for those two things is inexorable, everything is dying every five to 120 days. In other words, if you're not in the regrowth and repair mode for more than an hour or two a day, you'll be coming up short.

**Joan:** (to Dick) Your hormones must be pretty strong and your mind/body connection must be pretty much in balance, because you keep getting well!

**Dr. Cooke:** Aw, he's the bionic man! Here's something that's extremely important. In their treatment of medical problems, the Chinese never use the word "cancer." They say, "You've got a problem with your liver or your pancreas." That's it; they just say, "You've got a problem." The way we practice medicine here in the West, well, if you so much as just go to an oncologist's office, you'll die of fright! Seeing all the people in there sick and all that, they've got their porta-cath sticking out here … I mean, it doesn't look good! You're scared to death! So we have a problem in how we *talk* about medical problems. As physicians, we need to improve in this area. I've been in the hospital as a patient, and you don't like being talked to as "The Object." Nobody does.

The final door, or category, is exercise, because it is a natural metabolic enhancer. You increase the metabolic rate when you exercise. I tell people it's like tuning an instrument, because when you increase your metabolic rate, you increase sound cell communication, and all of your cells are all connected. That's body biochemistry—all the cells are connected and talking to each other. So when you exercise, you increase the metabolic rate, and the energy's burning, and they're all chattering together, as it were. However, a cancer cell does not communicate. The whole concept of receptor theory is pretty unfortunate, because actually, it's a good thing to have a receptor on a cancer cell. Cancer cells without them are really hard to deal with, because they lose what is called "natural contact envision" … cells are piled in multi-dimensions, and all are touching each other somewhere. So if intracellular communication ceases because you don't have receptors, hormones aren't going to talk to you, they're not going to get through to you, and then they're not going to talk to your neighbors. Then they begin to think they're the only cell and they have to start dividing to make more cells.

**Joan:** Do you think there's a secret behind why Dick always recovers?

**Dr. Cooke:** Well, I believe there are many factors. You have resilient physiology, and you've had some pretty good care. I think people need to hear stories like yours and to become more connected with themselves and less dependent on those "magic pills." Obviously, you have to take a number of drugs, which help you keep your heart healthy, and all the immuno-suppressive things that you take, your anti-rejection drugs, you're not going to *not* take those. I certainly don't blame you; I'd be taking them, too!

On the other hand, the lipids, or cholesterol-wasting drugs have many side effects, such as making it impossible for a man to make hormones. Since you only live on cholesterol, DHEA and 17 intermediates between that and testosterone, taking those away is like hobbling a horse and asking him to run. And a lot of people have "silent" heart attacks. Much of this is due to the fact that you use your muscles, and muscle re-growth and repair is severely impaired by those drugs, because they waste cholesterol—so you don't get as much testosterone. Even women who take them can have side effects. I interviewed a woman yesterday who's on Crestor—it's the only one she can take because it gives her the least amount of pain. She's a Pilates instructor, and when she teaches, she gets muscle pain. But this is not like the burn you're supposed to feel—it's a cramp.

Some of the anti-hypertension therapies could be revisited. For example, a lot of people have high blood pressure because they're nervous and have tremendous peripheral basal constriction. If they'd get a massage and relax more often, their blood pressure might come down to normal, but nobody suggests that. People who are overweight are carrying a burden that can make their heart have to work harder. There are a lot of little simple things that can be done. But we, as physicians, tend not to bring that up. Why? Because it means somebody has to work. First of all, the doctor must work to explain things to the patient; then the patient has to go home and decide to work and cooperate with their body. Everybody tends to say, "Please just give me a pill—I'd rather just take a pill."

**Joan:** What percentage of people do you think really do the work that doctors tell them to do?

**Dr. Cooke:** I think it's very low. I think as long as people are feeling pretty much all right, they figure, "Okay, I'm not going to look critically at what I'm doing." It's kind of like the lint on their life—they just don't want to be bothered with it. Let's face it, it's a pain in the ass to maintain a body, and the older you get, the more we all realize, "Oh my God, I've got to do this, I can't do that like I used to"… they sit home and complain, "Twenty years ago, I could do all this, now I can't do anything,"—well, that's because we're always changing. The essence of life is change, but that's not the expectation people have in this culture. They have the expectation, "If I do A, B, and C, I'm set." And they're willing to do A, B and C, but then they want to be set.

**Dick:** What can the average person do to improve their chances of living a longer life?

**Dr. Cooke:**    First of all, you have to cherish and take care of your body. There is a huge level of resistance to that, but that *is* the key to success. You have to accept what you have. For instance, I have low thyroid. I can whine about how I don't want to have it, but the truth of the matter is, I do. Along with that goes an overactive pancreas and a liver that's sluggish. So if I don't eat properly, I won't even be able to talk, and I might even pass out. I won't be able to operate a car; in general, I'll feel horrible. So would I like to have something different? Yes. But that's not happening.

A young woman called me the other day and said, "I'm just so tired of thinking about eating. What do you think of me just going on a ten-day fast?" I said, "You can try it, but I can tell you right now, you're going to feel like crashing and burning and like you're having a nervous breakdown, because you'll be so hypoglycemic you'll feel terrible and weak. Fasting is only for people who sit on the ground and pray, then pass out and wake up and pray some more. Otherwise, it doesn't work!" People have to come around to accepting what they have, and then seeking knowledge about how to work with it. In my experience, people in their teens and twenties, and people in their fifties and on up, are very anxious to do the work. It is the late twenties to fifty age range who cannot be bothered. They are looking for that "silver bullet" pill. I know so many people who are on not just one, two, or three antidepressants, but four! Half of this country's population, or maybe more, are just like Alice in Wonderland in that room, with all those jars of cookies. They're trying to eat the right cookies to get to be the right size to get through the keyhole. If you're stuck in that room, you're going to be on those cookies a long time! It isn't until people realize, "Well, maybe these cookies aren't good for me; maybe I should try something else," and they turn around and find there's another door they can leave through.

It isn't all centered around drugs. Drugs save lives; there are marvelous things we can do with the chemical manipulation that we've developed. The problem is that we're overly dependent on them now, and we're making people sick with them. I have a patient who's twelve years old—he's been on Adderall for hyperactivity since he was three. His teeth and hair are falling out and he looks like an emasculated choirboy. Everybody around him keeps thinking, "Oh, maybe there's another med that's going to help." But what goes up must come down, and I've heard these kids when they come crashing down. Did you know there are actually initiatives out there for school systems to be able to medicate children with antidepressants and other drugs without parental permission, if they feel it necessary? So yes, we need to be more vocal, and to figure out a safe forum in which to do that. What I have to say is very revolutionary. We need a revolution in our thinking in this population in order for us to preserve the health of our children and our planet. Like I say, once you start looking at the way the body is made, at body biochemistry, everything in the body is like the distilled essence of living life. If you can successfully live in the body, then you understand life enough to interact with other people and get along.

**Dick:**     So everybody needs to take a look at their body.

**Dr. Cooke:**     First, you have to be willing to be connected with your body, to look at it for what it is—not what it isn't. That's the Number One problem. You look in the mirror and want to see something else, so you start cutting here and there and whatever. That's the big problem.

**Dick:**       How does the average layman intelligently look at themselves with some degree of knowledge, without some kind of professional help?

**Dr. Cooke:**    Well, there are several simple things that you can look at. The five doors are not hard to deal with. Everybody eats, everybody can take vitamins. Everybody can make an effort, everybody can exercise. Hormone balance is difficult. It's a controversial issue because of the way the media has presented things. When the NIH published their studies years ago about Premarin, and the results showed that it didn't do *any* of the things it was marketed to do. It was marketed to prevent women from getting breast cancer, to prevent us from getting heart attacks. Well, they found that women on that drug actually had more instances of those things, not less. So the big to-do was, "Oh, my God, I'm not gonna take hormones anymore—they're bad for me!" The truth is that Premarin doesn't act in the same way as the estrogen that our bodies make. But because you can't patent something that's bio-identical, and money makes the world go round, people don't want to market bio-identical things or even talk about them, because they're not gonna make money. An oncologist was quoted in an NIH exposé, and I got so irritated with him, I called him up and was surprised that I got him. I said, "Of all the times you've been interviewed over the past few weeks, like by the *New York Times*, which has such a huge circulation, why did you never mentioned that this study was done on synthetic hormones and in no way is related to bio-identical hormones?" And he replied, "It's not newsworthy."

**Joan:** I read that! And the way they wrote the article, they didn't make a distinction, so everyone who read it thought, "All hormones are bad."

**Dr. Cooke:** Oh, I had people calling me right and left telling me they had to get off of this and that.

**Joan:** And they never talked about the fact that there was no research on Premarin! They never tried it on one woman, they just put it out there and it's been around now for 50 years.

**Dr. Cooke:** Well, even the fact that it caused uterine cancer, that was an "oh, well." Nobody bothered to look at female physiology and noticed that we only have high amounts of estrogen when we have progesterone in the system to balance. And we need that opposing balance thing there. So the thing is, they prescribed Premarin to all these women and it made them bleed profusely, and the uterine lining grew and they would bleed more; then they'd give them more Premarin, and pretty soon they'd either have to give them a hysterectomy to stop the bleeding or they developed uterine cancer! Eventually, they said, "Maybe we should be giving progesterone," and made a synthetic, Provera. To this day, I still meet women who are being prescribed Premarin without Provera, women who still have uteruses. In Canada, that's illegal.

**Dick**: Is there anything you recommend to anyone who has a loved one in the hospital, when it comes to being a caregiver or advocate?

**Dr. Cooke**: I would camp out and I would continually call for a second opinion, and fight for your loved one's right to be cared for properly. Because if you don't have someone to help you, you're probably not going to have a good result. The other thing is, if you're elderly, now they have these advanced directives in terms of what you want to have for long-term, extended care. But you have to watch people every minute. Because when mistakes are made on elderly patients, they just say, "Well, they're going to die soon, anyway. Let 'em go." If you're going to take the time and effort and money to operate upon someone, I feel that you need to stand behind them if they're salvageable, because it's your fault, you took them there. Even in Dick's case, I saved his life over the phone through Joan—more than once, actually. To me, that's disgusting.

**Dick**: Well, thank God you did!

**Dr. Cooke**: But the point is, it's ridiculous! He had sepsis from a deep-lying infection and the pulmonary fellow at that hospital, whom I actually talked to directly, said she thought it was just an allergy. And I said, "What? The man has a staph infection—that doesn't even matter! He's got streaking and redness up the arm. He has to be intubated and given high dose antibiotics, period."

**Dick**:         How did I stay alive, aside from the interventions you made? Why do you think I made it, and the next guy didn't?

**Dr. Cooke**:         Eventually, you did get connected with some very fine people. Your transplant surgeon and that whole team—they're excellent, they're professional and on top of things. I think that it was unfortunate that your lengthy preoperative wait for the heart was so rocky, but it's not atypical. I have watched patients die waiting for a heart, so I really think it's a miracle, Number One, that you got a heart at your age. And Number Two, that you made it through all these things. Now, even with these ridiculous complications that you had, you're able to survive. Your life is a gift.

**Dick**:         Do you make the gift, or do you just get it?

**Dr. Cooke**:         Well, I think it's kind of a two-way street. I think there are many gifts to be received, it's just whether you're willing to recognize them or not.

**Dick**:         I recognize them, every day, starting with this Joan. Any words of wisdom you want to pass on before we leave?

**Dr. Cooke**:         I just think we are coming into a time when there is still a tremendous amount of conflict in the arena of healthcare between those who want to make a lot of money and those who want to solve problems. Until the people who want to solve problems get more support, I think it's going to get worse. I hate to say that. I mean, yes, we want to keep patients out of the hospital. Why? Because people die in there! It's not as bad as it is in other parts of the world, it's just that here in the United States we are so used to having basically the Cadillac of care. Now we're inundated with so many other issues, like the nurses having to do too much paperwork; people who are trained to observe patients really aren't looking at them as much as they should be. There are a lot of problems, and a lot of sick people. People are living longer, and when they have problems and are not healthy, if they can't stay out of the hospitals, it becomes a vicious cycle.

The best advice is to be as healthy as you can and as independent as you can of drugs. Because you do have those five doors, and not one of them has the word drug on it, in my estimation. Yes, you can go to that medicine cabinet if you need to, to save a life. In that case, I will be the first person to say, "Go for it." But when the dust settles, it's always good to figure out the underlying problem. Why did the person get to this place, and what could we adjust so that the foundation is fixed? Get that figured out and then move on.

# Appendix Two:
# An Interview with Dr. Elkayam

The day Joan and I met with Dr. Uri Elkayam was definitely what you could call a "Red Letter Day"—it was a major positive turning point in my treatment, to put it mildly. This skilled physician is the director of the Heart Failure Program at the University of Southern California in Los Angeles. He has won numerous awards; he travels and lectures extensively around the world, is continuously involved in research and has been published many times over. You can learn more about his credentials and the amazing contributions he has made to the field of cardiology, research, and medicine by doing a Google search on his name. His background, expertise, and compassion make him a superb doctor, and he is a remarkable human being. Dr. Elkayam has been at USC since 1981, and has the well-deserved distinction of being listed in Best Doctors in America (2000-2008) and America's Top Doctors (2001-2008). He certainly proved to be an answer to prayer for us.

As I've mentioned, Joan was always vigilant, doing extensive research, and fortunately she paid very close attention when a new term was introduced to her, that of a "heart failure specialist." Here's her take on this:

**Joan:** In 2000, Dick had really severe heart failure. I mean, he couldn't walk from here to there. His cardiologist was in Orange County; all the doctors we'd ever had were here. Nobody had ever recommended a heart failure specialist. In fact, I had never heard of such a thing before. Well, the son of a friend of ours, Curt Harris, read an article in the *L.A. Times,* which he cut out for his father; it listed the names of three heart failure specialists in L.A. Our friend shared this valuable information with us. The cardiologists here in Newport Beach never said, "Why don't you go to a heart failure specialist in L.A.?" In fact, in thirty years, I can think of only one or two people who were referred by their doctor here in Orange County to a doctor in L.A. They just don't do it. They'll recommend somebody here, but sometimes there just isn't anyone. So we called all three of these heart failure specialists and decided we'd go to whoever could take him first. One was on vacation for a month, so I was told I could see his assistant. I asked, "How long has the assistant been around?" and the answer was, three years. That didn't sound like enough experience to us, so we kept dialing. The next one couldn't take him for a month. Dr. Elkayam could take us the following Monday, and he was at USC. We scheduled for Monday, and when we went in to see him, we brought all of Dick's medicines.

He spent two-and–a-half hours with us, and I don't even know if he gave him any new medicine; he just tweaked whatever he already had, saying, "Oh, that's too much of this, you can't put this with that," and so on. And the entire time, he was explaining everything. We were impressed and actually amazed—we'd never had a doctor take the time to explain everything, ever. Within 24 hours of following the new dosages, per Dr. Elkayam's advice, Dick was like a new person—it was a major chemical miracle type of thing. Dr. Elkayam kept him going for nine months like that, and then because Dick was at USC with him, he was able to get him into that hospital to wait for his transplant. We are so grateful we connected with this wonderful doctor.

When we interviewed him in March 2008, Dr. Elkayam was kind enough to share his insights on heart failure and transplantation today, with a look to the future. We asked what steered him toward specializing in the area of heart failure and to share some of his background.

**Dr. Elkayam:** After graduating medical school in Israel, I wanted to become an obstetrician, until I met a very charismatic physician who was trained in the United States and returned to Tel Aviv to head the cardiology department. I was the first intern in his Intensive Care Unit and I liked the work a lot, and he liked me so much that I decided to become a cardiologist. He also encouraged me to ask questions and try to answer them by doing research. Somehow, I was always fascinated by heart failure, and my research from the beginning has been mostly in this area. In the last three decades, my coworkers and I have performed more than 100 different studies, trying to better understand the mechanisms of the disease and develop new drugs and devices with the attempt to improve quality of life and prolong life of patients with heart failure. In the last 20 years, the area of heart failure and transplantation has become more complex, and it is best managed by heart failure specialists, i.e. cardiologists who have made a career decision devoted to heart failure. In fact, heart failure has become a subspecialty in cardiology. Very soon, physicians will have to take a board exam to be certified as specialists in heart failure and transplantation.

**Dick:**     Is it true that you try to get to people who are waiting for a heart but are not in the hospital—to help them survive longer without the operation?

**Dr. Elkayam:** Well, as you know, the operation is a perfect solution for very sick patients, but it may not be a good option for less sick patients for at least two reasons: one, it's very difficult to get hearts for less sick patients, and more importantly, by performing heart transplantation, we're replacing one condition by another, since lifestyle after transplantation is not completely normal. It involves frequent visits to the doctor, having regular biopsies, taking multiple medications, some of them with side effects. For all these reasons, heart transplantation is not something that one should rush into, and every effort should be made to delay transplantation without risking the patient life. We are fortunate that, because of the development of effective therapy and the increasing skill of physicians, we can stabilize even sick patients and thus delay the operation. And since you were on the list several years ago, Dick, we have made even more progress, and we have developed a better understanding and ability to further delay the process. We are more aggressive medically, and new therapeutic options are currently available to patients that were not available when you were waiting for heart transplantation.

Heart failure is defined as an inability of the heart to contract or relax normally. The leading causes for heart failure are heart attacks, high blood pressure, valvular heart disease, aging, and excessive consumption of alcohol, as well as the use of illicit drugs such as cocaine and amphetamines. In many cases, the heart is not only contracting poorly, but the contraction of its different parts in not synchronized. That means that all parts of the heart are not contracting at the same time, and when some are contracting, others are relaxing, resulting in an inefficient work of the heart and more heart failure. In the last several years, we have learned to synchronize the heart function by placing two leads in the heart, one activating each wall; the activation occurs at the same time, resulting in improvement of the heart function. Today, we are able to stabilize patients to the point that they can be taken off the waiting list for heart transplantation. Most of the patients who have heart transplants are very sick and have to be hospitalized while they are waiting for donor heart. The frequency of performing heart transplant on patients waiting on the list at home has deceased.

**Dick:**      Would you call that practice of delaying the absolute need for surgery the primary thrust of your practice?

**Dr. Elkayam:**  Well, transplantation is basically one way of dealing with heart failure. But my emphasis is on the other way which is the art of using multiple medications, trying to achieve harmony between them, and the use of new devices that can improve symptoms and prevent sudden death. You can really do extremely well today with medications and devices, especially in an educated patient, so that transplantation can be postponed until the patient develops severe illness that requires the operation. I should also mention the implantable defibrillator, a small device like a pacemaker, implanted within the heart and able to detect life threatening arrhythmias and terminate them by delivering an electrical shock. This device saves many lives.

**Dick**: Hallelujah! Yeah, if you don't mind getting knocked down once in awhile!

**Dr. Elkayam**: Right! Everything has its down side.

**Dick**: What do you think are the biggest challenges facing healthcare in heart disease for the future?

**Dr. Elkayam**: Unfortunately, the number of patients with heart failure is growing dramatically and the trend is expected to continue for a number of reasons. The first is the increasing age of the population. People live longer, and the aging of the heart often results in the development of heart failure. In addition, the better care we can provide has resulted in survival of patients with heart attacks, diabetes and high blood pressure. Such patients may have some damage to the heart which, over time, leads to enlargement of the heart and eventually to heart failure. How are we going to manage all the patients with heart failure? The answer is probably prevention and education. It is hard to manage heart failure and prevent hospitalizations when people don't take their medication, or don't follow a healthy diet. Our statistics show that about 50 percent of patients who become sick enough to be hospitalized for heart failure will be hospitalized again at least once within the first year. The mortality in patients who are hospitalized for worsening heart failure is about 20 to 30 percent per year. It's actually worse than most forms of cancer.

One of the most severe problems we are facing in this country is the overcrowding of hospitals. I hear from some of my patients and friends that most emergency rooms are crowded and some hospitals cannot accommodate a sick patient, who has to be sent to another hospital. This hospital crowding will affect the life of all of us. That's why I truly believe that people in the community, especially those with financial means, should use hospitals as target of donation in order to improve the quality of life of people in the community.

**Dick:** I've heard that the wait in the ER can be up to two hours.

**Dr. Elkayam:** A recent article has reported a wait of one-and-a-half hours in the ER for patients who came in with heart attack. This is unbelievable and very dangerous. Another concern related to patient healthcare is the escalating cost of medicine—which is good, in a way, because it means we're getting better care. When someone comes to the hospital with a bad headache, the likelihood of getting an MRI is high and the chance of missing a major problem is low. Today, we don't tolerate any uncertainty; we demand the best care, and it costs a lot of money. I believe that the biggest challenge faced by the present politicians is how to control the escalating cost of medicine and at the same time provide the high level of care that people in this country want and deserve. For example, an AICD (defibrillator), which can be lifesaving and is indicated in patients with heart failure, costs $30,000 or $40,000.

**Dick:** What about the future? Anything looming in terms of heart transplantation?

**Dr. Elkayam:** Transplantation is always going to be offered to only a limited number of patients with heart failure, because of the shortage of donor hearts. In a way, it's good news, since it shows that we're doing a good job in protecting people who get involved in accidents from head injuries. But when it comes to the number of patients who could benefit from heart transplantation, there's always going to be a shortage. The number of people with heart failure is huge, and only a small fraction can get a heart transplant. There are a number of new innovations that will help very sick patients with heart failures; first, our surgeons are much more successful now at performing bypass surgery and valve surgery in patients who have bad hearts. We are developing new surgical procedures that can remove damaged heart muscles and improve the function of the heart. We're developing valves that are inserted over a catheter without opening the chest, to be used in patients with severe heart failure where surgery is associated with high risk. In addition, there is a new generation of devices that work as pumps and can support the failing heart in patients who are not candidates for heart transplantation. Furthermore, there are new devices that are implanted within the heart and provide a great deal of information, such as the pressures within the heart, the heart rhythm, content of fluid in the lungs, and even how much activity the patient is doing. These devices allow for remote monitoring and should help to achieve better communication between the patient and the physician.

**Dick:** So one of the big opportunities is to continue to find techniques and assistance to keep the patient from having to have a transplant?

**Dr. Elkayam:** I think we're doing a good job with that now. We have patients with fairly bad hearts who have lived for years without transplantation. You have a small percentage of the heart failure population who are getting transplants. So it's like a pyramid with the small number of patients at the top getting a transplant, and the majority of patients with heart failure that are to be treated successfully by other means—and these means are improving all the time.

**Dick:** Any basic advice for someone who thinks they have the beginnings of heart problems?

**Dr. Elkayam:** It is important to detect heart disease early and prevent its progression and the development of heart failure. An echocardiogram can detect early decrease in heart function and the presence of valvular disease. Stress tests, with or without imaging such as echocardiogram and radionuclide tests, can provide early detection of coronary artery disease. Early diagnosis of heart disease allows the use of medications, which are very effective in slowing down the progression of the disease. The use of such medications and lifestyle modification is extremely important. For a compliant patient, the outcome of aggressive medical therapy is often comparable to than that of angioplasty or surgery. I think most of us now understand the value of preventing heart disease and we put far more emphasis on it.

**Dick:** You really made a huge difference when I first came to see you, just by juggling my medications around, adjusting the dosages and so on.

**Dr. Elkayam:** Yes, the key for success in managing a patient with severe heart failure is having the right temperament, being patient, working with the patient and family, and finding the right formula of the appropriate therapy. Not every physician is able to have the time for that. For these reasons, more and more medical centers have a dedicated heart failure center that specializes in the treatment of patient with heart failure.

**Dick:** You and your staff were a blessing to me. I haven't had a single rejection.

**Dr. Elkayam:** That's great. The majority of the people don't have rejections; that's the beauty of it. But when there is a rejection, it's usually earlier rather than later after the transplantation and it can be risky.

**Dick:** Well, I think the message we want to put forth in the book is that the patients need to jump on preventative measures and become educated. Where are you headed next?

**Dr. Elkayam:** That's a good question. We have a lot of work to do and have been involved in a number of research programs with an attempt to develop new and better treatment of heart failure. In the last several years, we have also been investigating a fascinating disease called peripartum cardiomyopathy. This is a potentially devastating condition where young women, who are otherwise healthy, become pregnant and then develop severe heart failure. Ten percent of these patients actually either die or have heart transplantation. Having heart transplantation at the age of 25 is obviously much worse than having it at the age of 69. Fortunately, this condition is uncommon and occurs in one of 2,500 deliveries, but the incidence keeps increasing as women become pregnant at older ages. We have been able to review the records of many of these patients and develop the largest database in the world with this disease, and to help many of these patients. We intend to continue to investigate this disease, to try to understand the cause and develop effective therapy that hopefully will prevent the major complications often associated with this condition. The diagnosis of peripartum cardiomyopathy is often delayed, since the last thing people think about is heart failure in a young woman who always has been healthy. About fifty percent of the patients are diagnosed late, and some develop severe complications such as strokes, severe heart failure, and even death, all of which are preventable. We are on the mission to increase the awareness of this disease and make sure that most of these patients will be diagnosed early and receive the appropriate treatment.

We also have been involved in the development of new, implantable devices that are capable of transmitting information that can guide the patients and their physicians into providing appropriate care. These new capabilities allow us to determine, for example, how active the patient is. So if the activity decreases, something may be wrong. We can actually measure the water content in the chest and diagnose congestion even before the patient develops symptoms. I am very excited about the future.

There are many challenges that we need now to learn how to utilize this available technology for the benefit of our patients. All these capabilities that are available will keep me busy for the next two decades, before I decide to retire.

**Dick:** I don't understand how you handle the tremendous load … my doctors follow me about once every six weeks, and I see them about three or four times a year. When you add that up with the number of patients, it's a tremendous aftercare load.

**Dr. Elkayam:** Yes, it is, and we need the manpower to do that, especially since the number of patients with heart failure keeps increasing. At the same time, I am optimistic that, with all the new innovations in diagnosis and therapy, patients with heart failure will have a better and longer life.

# Appendix Three:
# An Interview with Dr. Weaver

We later talked with Dr. Fred Weaver, a wonderful vascular surgeon at USC who "saved my bacon" when I had the blood clot situation in my thigh/groin area. He very graciously did an interview with us, which contains some good information. We have paraphrased it and share it with you now.

Dr. Weaver equates his job to that of a plumber, in that he "takes care of the pipes" (the blood vessels, veins and arteries) in the body. He explained that when our "pipes" get too much rust or junk in them, so to speak, there are a variety of chemicals and drugs that can help to clean them out. Aspirin and Plavix are two of the drugs that he included in the category of lubricating the pipes, keeping debris from forming on the wall. Should the pipes become so clogged that they develop blockages that prevent those lubricants from doing do the trick, however, then it's time to "re-plumb" in other ways, such as going the surgical route.

The coronary arteries can be affected by the same diseases as any of the other blood vessels—the most common disease in the U.S. is atherosclerosis, which affects every blood vessel in the body to varying degrees. The coronary vessels tend to be the most involved with this particular disease.

Dr. Weaver went on to explain, "Heart attacks are by far the most common vascular event. You simply clog the artery and lose a portion of the heart muscle because it dies, due to the fact it has insufficient blood flow, and that's the basic definition of a heart attack. It also affects the carotids, the legs, and the arteries to the kidneys and the intestines. It may also destroy the structural integrity of the wall of the vessel, and that creates an aneurism. So that is the disease process. It's a systemic disease; once it's discovered in one vascular area, it's important to keep looking for it in all of the others, since there's a significant percentage where other areas coexist. It may be silent until there's a catastrophe. Quite frequently, it is."

We asked him what the layman's terminology would be of what happened when the clots broke loose in my groin area. His response was that my condition was one of having "thrombosed," or clotted, the blood vessels that went to my lower extremities. So that situation was not actually atherosclerosis, which is more of a chronic condition; it was an acute thrombosis, or a large amount of blood clots. The procedure Dr. Weaver and his team did on me is called a "thrombectomy"; they cleaned out the area, and then did a femur-to-femur bypass, to create better blood flow from one leg to the other.

Because of Dr. Weaver's vast knowledge and experience in his area of expertise, we questioned him about what advice he had to offer to help avoid heart problems. This was his response:

"Vascular health—a big term these days—is the maintenance of your blood vessels. My advice is to do the best job possible with your own maintenance and to take an anti-coagulant agent, which can be as simple as aspirin. Aspirin affects the ability of the bloodstream to stop little areas of bleeding, which occur all the time in the body. It's kind of a little maintenance mechanism that plugs all the little holes that occur over the course of a day. It's been shown that if you take one aspirin a day, it decreases that ability to clog a bit, so the debris doesn't build up in the vessels quite as much, and it definitely decreases the risk of heart attack and cardiovascular events. So one aspirin a day, just in general, is a good idea for anybody. Some people can't tolerate a regular 325 milligram-strength aspirin. There are coated ones, but if someone needs a lower dosage, then 81 milligrams definitely has a beneficial effect as well. Other kinds of things that are important for blood vessel maintenance are the statin medications, such as Lipitor. They are prescribed now not only for heart problems and high cholesterol, but in general, the statins have the benefit of decreasing plaque formation as well as seeming to stabilize what existing plaque is there, so that it doesn't progress or rupture or create catastrophic problems."

We went on to discuss how there is a controversy about statin drugs these days. Dr. Weaver told us that they can cause problems with the liver in a relatively small percentage of people. His basic take on statin agents is that, in general, he believes them to be excellent; however, their side effects are difficult for some people to tolerate. He went on to mention some non-statin agents that may be substituted in some cases with lesser side effects, such as Zetia and Vytorin.

Next, we asked him what the average person can do to prevent vascular problems. He told us that if someone has diabetes, high blood pressure, high cholesterol, or is a smoker, those are four major risk factors for vascular disease, including heart problems. The other issues to look at are just genetics and your own family history, because those can have a whole lot to do with vascular disease. For example, if your father or mother had coronary problems or an aortic aneurism, you have a very high chance of having that as well. So much of this, in particular cholesterol metabolism, is already pre-programmed through the genetic code, and if you've got family members with a history, your risk of having those kinds of problems is clearly increased.

Dick brought up the fact that he and Joan have a good friend who is a former vascular surgeon who is adamant that there's a tendency toward too much amputation as opposed to surgeons who are skilled in Dr. Weaver's field. He said his partner has recently studied national databases of acute emergency settings (like Dick's clot situation). Over the course of the last ten years, there's actually been a definite decrease in the incidence of amputation. Concurrently, there has been an increase in the use of balloons, stents, and chemicals to treat problems of this nature.

Joan inquired as to Dr. Weaver's best advice for patients coming into the hospital with any kind of a problem, and Dick immediately suggested, "Have a blonde, good-looking wife who is very pushy!" Dr. Weaver actually agreed that, to some extent, that is very good advice. He stressed several times that having an advocate who is going to push for you, as Joan has done for Dick many times, is one of the best possible scenarios. He explained,

"If you look at it from an emergency room perspective, emergency rooms are understaffed, underfunded, and overwhelmed. All they deal with is acute problems. When somebody comes in with an acute catastrophe such as Dick's, they're sitting there trying to get attention along with all of these other people who are there for relatively mundane things. A patient who is in agony simply cannot wait for hours. So a family member who is an advocate, and who will not take "no" for an answer, is actually a very important thing. There are times when family members can get themselves too involved, but not in the sense that their loved one is receiving adequate attention. It's one thing when they try to get involved with all the medical management questions, but it's another thing when they can go, "Hey, *look*! His legs are blue, he hurts—something has to be done *now*, we need to get going on this!" And things such as contacting doctors who know about who you are crucial. There's no substitute for doctors knowing your medical issues and medical history. Because that emergency doc is seeing you for the first time. Particularly for someone like Dick, who would be coming in with a heart transplant, there's no way the doctor is going to be able to get all that medical history together in that short time in the ER."

We touched upon the topic of how he feels the medical and healthcare system in general could be improved. He opined that, in a very general sense, patients and physicians have become too separated. He has observed that a large portion of that has to do with the way compensation and payment occurs (with insurance), and that he feels it's necessary to find a way to return to creating a relationship between the physician and patient. He was quick to add, "The U.S. has the greatest healthcare system in the world. I think politicians and other people with different agendas tend to point out how we're deficient in this and that; but the reality is that people still come here from other countries seeking healthcare."

Joan explained how embarrassing it was for her not to have an updated medication list on her person when Dick went in for the blood clot episode, and because he was wearing his shorts, he didn't have his wallet with his list. Even after all they'd been through medically at that point, she still didn't have a copy of the list and didn't know the current dosages.

Dr. Weaver agreed that those are great points, and reiterated that family members are the best advocates, because what loving family members can and will provide is simply far superior to the advocacy efforts of surrogates. The doctor expounded that whenever he has a patient dealing with a situation comparable to the magnitude of Dick's clot surgery, if they don't have a supportive family to go back to, they typically end up going to a nursing home and never getting out. His closing comment was, "Family is everything when it comes to bringing somebody back to stable health."

# Useful Organizations/Web-Sites

The Association of Organ Procurement Organization (AOPO)
www.aopo.org/aopoindex.asp
136 Beverly Road, Suite 100
McLean, VA 22101
Phone: 703-556-4242 Fax: 703-556-4852

American Society of Transplantation
www.a-s-t.org
15000 Commerce Parkway, Suite C
Mt. Laurel, NJ 08054
Phone: 856-439-9982 Fax: 859-439-9982

National Transplant Society—Register online to become an organ donor.
www.organdonor.org
3149 Dundee Road, Suite 314
Northbrook, IL 60062

Organ Procurement and Transplantation Network (OPTN)
Data citing website.
www.optn.org
Post Office Box 2484
Richmond, VA 23218

*Richard and Joan Stevens*

Organ Donation Campaign
www.rayma.com.my/giftoflife/signup.html

The National Marrow Donor Program
www.marrow.org

# Alternateive Care

**Table-Tipping**
Valynda Dupré—Transformational Life Coach, Spiritual Healer, Teacher and Multiple Modality Therapist
Valynda@gentletruth.com
Phone: 602-765-1109

**Medical Intuitive**
Susan Klopstein
Phone: 949-854-1085

# Caregivers & Caregiving Books

Canfield, Jack; Mark Victor Hansen and LeAnn Thieman, eds. *Chicken Soup for the Caregiver's Soul: Stories to Inspire Caregivers in the Home, the Community and the World.* Deerfield Beach, FL: HCI, 2004.

Barg, Gary. *The Fearless Caregiver: How to Get the Best Care for Your Loved One and Still Have a Life of Your Own.* Sterling, VA: Capital Books, 2003.

Hennessey, Maya. *If Only I'd Had This Caregiving Book.* Bloomington, IN: Authorhouse, 2006.

Samples, Pat; and Diane and Marvin Larsen. *Self-Care for Caregivers: A Twelve Step Approach.* Center City, MN: Hazelden, 2000.

American Association of Retired Persons (AARP)
www.aarp.org
601 E Street NW
Washington, DC 20049
Phone: 1-888-OUR-AARP

Caregiver Resource Center
www.caregiveroc.org
St. Jude Centers for Rehabilitation and Wellness
2767 E. Imperial Hwy.,
2nd Floor
Brea, CA 92821
Phone: 800-543-8312; 714-870-3530

National Council on Aging (NCOA)
www.NCOA.org
1901 L Street, N.W.
4th floor
Washington, D.C. 20036
Phone: 202-479-1200 Fax: 202-479-0735

# Bibliography

Barnard, Christiaan. *One Life.* New York: Macmillan, 1970.

----------*The Second Life: Memoirs.* Cape Town: Vlaeberg, 1993.

Downs, Marion P. *Shut Up and Live! (You Know How).* Brentwood, TN: Cold Tree Press, 2005.

Fine, Laura L. *Laura's New Heart: A Healer's Spiritual Journey through a Heart Transplant.* Bloomington, IN: 1st Books Library, 2004.

Green, Reg. *The Gift That Heals: Stories of Hope, Renewal And Transformation through Organ and Tissue Donation.* Bloomington, IN: Authorhouse, 2007.

Hay, Louise. *You Can Heal Your Life.* Santa Monica: Hay House, 1987.

Hermans, Janet. *Perfect Match: A Kidney Transplant Reveals the Ultimate Second Chance.* Longwood: FL, Xulon, 2006.

Klug, Chris, and Steve Jackson. *To the Edge and Back: My Story from Organ Transplant Survivor to Olympic Snowboarder.* New York: Carol & Graf, 2004.

Moose, Candace C. *The Grateful Heart: Diary of a Heart Transplant.* Cold Spring Harbor, NY: Rosalie Ink Publications, 2005.

Morgentaler, Abraham, MD. *Testosterone for Life: Recharge Your Vitality, Sex Drive, Muscle Mass and Overall Health.* New York: McGraw-Hill, 2008.

Nance, Lisa Stiles. *Life in Limbo: Waiting for a Heart Transplant.* New York: iUniverse, 2003.

Parr, Elizabeth, Ph.D., and Mize, Janet, R.N. *Coping with an Organ Transplant: A Practical Guide.* New York: Avery, 2001.

Pearsall, Paul. *The Heart's Code: Tapping the Wisdom and Power of Our Heart Energy.* New York: Broadway, 1998.

Shaw, Gaea. *Dying to Live: From Heart Transplant to Abundant Life.* Longmont, CO: Pilgrims Process, Inc., 2005.

Siemers, Nancy. *Stories of the Heart: Reflections on the Heart Transplant Journey: Stories of Hope and Inspiration.* Minneapolis: Kirk House Publishers, 1999.

Claire, Sylvia, and William Novak. *A Change of Heart: A Memoir.* Boston: Little Brown, 1997.

Tilney, Nicholas L. *Transplant: From Myth to Reality.* New Haven: Yale University Press, 2003.

Yomtoob, Parichehr; Laura Yomtoob and Deborah Weppler. *The Gift of Life 2: Surviving the Waiting List and Liver Transplantation.* Deerfield, IL: Rainbow International Press, 2005.

# References & Media Articles

"A Question of How to Ration Life." *Los Angeles Times* November 2006: A34.

Alexander, Max. "Night Shift Nightmare." *Reader's Digest* June 2007: 113-120.

"Angioplasty: Resist the Rush." *On Health* March 2007 Vol. 9 No. 3: 1, 4-5

"Bad Bugs." *Forbes.* June 2006: 62, 64, 67-68.

Bernhard, Blythe. "A Matter of Life or Death." *Orange County Register* 7 March 2006: 3.

Bernhard, Blythe. "Organ Donor Shortage." *Orange County Register* March 2006.

Bernhard, Blythe, and Chris Knap. "Waiting in the Dark: Patients on UCI's Liver-Transplant List." *Orange County Register* December 2006.

Bernhard, Blythe. "'What If' Hangs over Loved Ones." *Orange County Register* November 2005.

Bernhard, Blythe. "Hospital Chose to Continue Transplants." *Orange County Register* December 2005.

Bernhard, Blythe. "UCI Liver-Transplant Program Lacked Surgeons, Not Organs." *Orange County Register* December 2005.

Brink, Susan. "It's Never Just One Thing That Leads to Serious

Error." *Los Angeles Times* 28 January 2007: F1, F6.

Brown, David. "Medical System Is Ready To Collapse." *Sign on San Diego* June 2006.

Chavez, Erika. "A Gift from the HEART." *Los Angeles Times* 20 February 2008: Life Wellness pgs 1 & 2.

Chung, Juliet. "System Helps Organ Donors Sign Up." *Los Angeles Times* July 2006: B4.

Cool, Lisa Collier. "It Was Worth Taking a Risk to Save a Life." *O, The Oprah Magazine* November 2004: 271.

Flynn, Sean. "How to Survive Your Local ER." *Parade* October 2006: 4-6.

Forbes, Steve. "Open-Heart Surgery–90% Off!" *Forbes* August 2007: 21-2.

Gallagher, Karin. "12 Steps to Becoming a Better Patient." *Orange Coast* January 2007, 88, 90-3.

"Get Better Care from Your Doctor." *Consumer Reports* February 2007: 32-9.

Gleason, Jim. "A Gift from The Heart" www.transweb.org/people/recips/experien/gleason February 03, 2005.

Grady, Denise. "Doing Battle with the Insurance Company in a Fight to Stay Alive." *New York Times* July 2009: 19.

Grady, Denis. "Cancer Patients, Lost in a Maze of Uneven Care." *New York Times*

July 2009: 1, 18.

Grassinger, Marysue, and Kristine Schonder. "Managing Side Effects of Immunosuppressant Medications." *LifeTimes Magazine* Issue 4, 1999.

Green, Jan. "Patient, Protect Thyself." *Los Angeles Times* 28 January 2007: F1, F6.

"Guarding against Stroke." *OnHealth* May 2007: 4-5.

"Having Surgery? What You Need To Know." *Agency for Healthcare Research and Quality* October 2005.

HealthGrades Fifth Annual Health Grades Hospital Quality And Clinical Excellence Study. *HealthGrades* January 2007: 1-48.

Healy, Melissa. "The Changing Rules of Organ Donation." *Los Angeles Times* November 2004: F1, F4.

"Heart to Heart." *Transplant Connection* November 2004: 268-270, 294.

Kahn, Jennifer. "Mending Broken Hearts." *National Geographic* February 2007: 40-64.

Kapadia, Reshma. "10 Things Your Hospital Won't Tell You." *SmartMoney* October 2006: 112-14.

Kirchheimer, Sid. "Are You Being Overcharged for Medical Care?" *Bottom Line Health* Vol. 27 No. 14: 1-2 .

Neergaard, Lauran. "Drug Error Rampant." *Orange County Register* July 2006: News 10.

Ornstein, Charles. "Many Kidneys Turned Down at UCI." *Los Angeles Times* January 2006: B1,B10.

Oz, Mehmet C., MD. "Get Better Care from Your Doctor." *Bottom Line Health*

September 2006: 9-11.

Phillips, William G. "My Father's Life; Organ Donor Real Life Story" *Men's Health* December 2006: 164-9.

Reeve, Dana. "Actress Excelled in Role as Caregiver, Advocate." *Los Angeles Times* 8 March 2006: A10.

Stevens, Lise M. "Organ Donation." *JAMA Patient Page* July 2001 Vol. 208, No. 1

"The Most Dangerous Medical Mistake." *Parade* April 2007: 16.

White, Lawrence E. "Equity Debate Won't Get Me A Kidney" *Orange County Register* 22 July 2007: 1,5.

Zarembo, Alan. "Inequality / Death by Geography." *Los Angeles Times* June 2006: A1, A28-A29.

# Author Biographies

## Richard Stevens

Richard Stevens is one of the top resort and hospitality executives in the world. In his forty years as a corporate turnaround specialist, he ran multimillion-dollar projects for the Howard Hughes organization and oil tycoon Jack Wrather, founder of the Disneyland Hotel resort in Anaheim. His resume includes directing marina development projects in Miami, Los Angeles, Mexico and Japan; running a professional football team in L.A.; and heading up the 1984 Olympic Pentathlon event. He also engineered the creation of one of California's most successful vacation destinations, the Spruce Goose-Queen Mary attractions, which have drawn more than one million visitors a year.

A graduate of University of California, Berkeley, Stevens served as a regular Army officer in the Korean War and later was assigned to direct one of the largest logistics bases in the Pacific theatre—a $400 million electronics supply operation.

Stevens took over the famous-but-money-losing Balboa Bay Club in Newport Beach when he was thirty-three, and then financed and built apartments, tennis courts and spa facilities, making it a financial success. He expanded the resort, creating waterfront condos on the shores of Catalina Island and developing the Balboa Bay Club in Palm Springs. Partnering with Jack Wrather, he also served as president of the Disneyland Hotel.

Stevens bought the 495,000-acre Cabin Bar Ranch in 1979 and developed its spring water resources in association with Anheuser Busch and later, Crystal Geyser. He and his wife owned the famed Jockey Club in Miami in the years prior to taking over the helm of the Fisher Island Club, a failing, $500 million luxury resort and marina nearby, that was losing several million per year.

When Stevens successfully resurrected Fisher Island, the *Miami Herald* wrote, "Dick Stevens is one of the world's leading authorities and executives in the resort, club, marina and hospitality industries. His more than thirty-five years experience in creating and operating some of the most prestigious waterfront facilities in America is a testament to his vision and skills as both a manager and entrepreneur."

He was appointed by California Governor George Deukmejian to the board of the California State Exposition and Fair Expo committee, and when his colleagues elected him chairman of the Expo, the *Orange County Register* reported: "Richard Stevens has taken on some monumental business enterprises, any of which would constitute a memorable career. Stevens played key roles in the making of The Balboa Bay Club, The Disneyland Hotel, The Queen Mary and the Spruce Goose into what they are today. He also ran the 1984 Olympics Pentathlon competition."

Stevens recently sold his company, The Bellport Group, which planned, developed, and managed marinas in the U.S., Mexico, and Japan. He is currently chairman of his personal investment company, Recreational Advisors International, and lives in Newport Beach, California with his wife and co-author, Joan.

## Joan Stevens

Joan was born in the Midwest and grew up in the Cleveland area. Her father owned a grocery store where Joan worked. She attended Ohio State University and subsequently returned to Cleveland to work as an administrative assistant to a prominent lawyer/developer for many years. Joan married and had two children, Lisa and Brad Leine. The family moved to Southern California in 1971.

She subsequently started the Pro Shop at the famous John Wayne Tennis Club. Joan became active in real estate investments for her own account and has been active for thirty years.

In 1977, she married Richard Stevens, and for more than thirty years has worked with him as a partner in his many business adventures.

Just two years after they were married, Dick was stricken with heart disease. That was the beginning of a twenty-eight year journey in Joan's dealing, out of necessity, with the continuing demands of keeping her husband alive. She continues in that capacity to this date and is the undisputed captain of the Stevens' health team.

# A special note to you from Joan Stevens

Dear Friend,

And we are friends, because we've shared quite the journey together!

As you know, everything to do with health care is constantly changing. Hospitals, insurance, forms of treatment, mainstream acceptance of non-traditional approaches to healing...nothing stays the same day-to-day.

In order to maintain our health, and in order to stay on top of trends, Dick and I are constantly reading new material, going online, interviewing experts, and consulting with physicians and alternative health practitioners.

We would like to share with you the benefits of our continued explorations. You are welcome to visit our website, www.JoansClub. com, and sign up to subscribe to our blog, which will provide you with cutting-edge information about everything to do with health and longevity.

There is no charge for the newsletter, because we believe that individuals informed with the latest knowledge can make the best decisions for themselves. And in today's world, don't fool yourself—you, not your doctor or your surgeon, are your own primary health care provider. You're in charge. That's the philosophy of this book, and the blog is a means of keeping that conversation going.

I hope you'll join that conversation by visiting www.JoansClub. com, signing up for the blog, and adding your own comments, experiences, and knowledge base to the site. Write to us at info@ JoansClub.com. We look forward to meeting you!

Sincerely,

Joan Stevens